ANTI-KOMMUNISM IN LATIN AMERICA

BOOKS BY JUAN JOSÉ ARÉVALO

Viajar es Vivir (To Travel Is to Live) Buenos Aires, 1933

Distancia, Conocimiento, Intimidad. Ensayo Gnoseológico (Distance, Knowledge, Intimacy. A Gnosiological Essay) Guatemala, 1935

Cinco Centavos de Axiología (Five Cents Worth of Axiology) (The Science of Values) Guatemala, 1936

La Pedagogía de la Personalidad (The Pedagogy of Personality) La Plata, Argentina, 1937

La Filosofía de los Valores en la Pedagogía (The Philosophy of Values in Pedagogy) Buenos Aires, 1939

Istmania: Tierras del Istmo (Istmania: the Lands of the Isthmus) Guatemala, 1945; Buenos Aires, 1954

Las Cuatro Raíces del Servilismo. Ensayo de Interpsicología (The Four Roots of Servility. Essay on Interrelated Psychology) Guatemala, 1945

Escritos Pedagógicos y Filosóficos (Writings on Pedagogy and Psychology) Guatemala, 1945

Escritos Políticos y Discursos Presidenciales (Political Writings and Presidential Speeches) Havana, 1953

Guatemala: La Democracia y el Imperio (Guatemala: Democracy and the Empire) Santiago de Chile, 1954; Montevideo, Mexico, and Tel Aviv, 1955; definitive final edition, Buenos Aires, 1955

Fábula del Tiburón y las Sardinas. América Latina Estrangulada. (Fable of the Shark and the Sardines. The Strangling of Latin America) Buenos Aires, 1956; Havana, 1961; English edition [The Shark and the Sardines], New York: Lyle Stuart, 1961

Anti-
KOMMUNISM
IN
LATIN AMERICA

An X-Ray of the Process Leading to a New Colonialism

by JUAN JOSÉ ARÉVALO
former President of Guatemala

Translated from the Spanish by Carleton Beals

Lyle Stuart Inc.   New York

Anti-Kommunism in Latin America

© 1963 by Juan José Arévalo

Library of Congress Catalog Card Number 63-7912

Queries regarding rights and permissions
    should be addressed to Lyle Stuart
    at 239 Park Avenue South,
    New York, N. Y. 10003

Translated by Carleton Beals from the
second edition of *AntiKomunismo En América Latina,*
1959, published by Editorial Palestra,
Buenos Aires

Typography by Polyglot Press
Editorial Supervision by Eileen Brand
Published by Lyle Stuart Inc.
Printed in the United States of America

TABLE OF CONTENTS

INTRODUCTION

Guiseppe Garibaldi set out to free Italy with seven armed men and a mule. At the end of March, 1963, after seven years of exile, former President of Guatemala Juan José Arévalo returned to his country to free it from dictatorship—without any armed men and without a mule.

Garibaldi had a long bitter struggle to sweep out foreign invaders and petty tyrants. But within twenty-four hours of Arévalo's arrival to announce his candidacy for the November, 1963, elections, Dictator Miguel Ydígoras was flying into exile in Nicaragua.

Unfortunately the Guatemalan coup in no way represented liberation. Rather it was a further tightening of existing military brutality over a land already long mangled and trampled upon. The gorilla chewing up the little banana kingdom with his tanks and guns is General Enrique Peralta (Ydígoras' own Minister of War). He is a creature well trained in the United States for such monkeyshines (i.e., how to administer the local police state), and has been provided by our authorities with an over-kill supply of weapons and planes.

The reason for the armed coup is a *reductio ad absurdum* of the McCarthy mind. Dictator Ydígoras was "too soft on Communism." Yet Ydígoras had been perhaps the most conspicuous, ranting anti-Communist in the hemisphere. He had been the ideal yes-man for the United

States office of colonial affairs, which is misnamed the Organization of American States and is largely made up of representatives of the local police states dutifully rubber-stamping Washington orders. Ydígoras had hung by his tail, making grimaces and threats.

Actually there were few Communists in Guatemala; they had been killed, jailed, or exiled. So were the leaders of all other independent parties—all except leaders of a small Catholic Party and Ydígoras' own little party (which was unable to win an election even though 75 per cent of the voters had been disenfranchised and the polls were presided over by bayonets). All labor, peasant, teacher, and other civic organizations had been destroyed. But he was "soft on Communism." And so a bigger gorilla now hangs by his tail, making wider grimaces, shouting worse epithets at Communism, and crunching the banana republic in his big teeth.

The real fear, of course, was of Arévalo who, having been the first president to do something for the people since Rufino Barrios a hundred years ago, was bound to be elected right in the teeth of the bayonets. The elections had to be prevented at all costs.

It is precisely with this fraudulent anti-Communism in the Latin American police states that Arévalo's book deals so competently. Nothing points up the truth of this book better than the seizure of power by Peralta in Guatemala. Those who have read Arévalo's previous magnificent and fearless book, *The Shark and the Sardines* (Lyle Stuart, 1961), already know his brilliant style, his uncompromising thought, his hard-hitting truths, always wrapped in the silk of irony and satire. It was one of the few books ever published in this country giving the viewpoint of the

10

Latin American people rather than that of the State Department and its dutiful yes-men rulers of South America. Now in *Anti-Kommunism in Latin America,* Arévalo once more displays his brilliance and insight.

The present volume was first brought to my attention in 1961 in Buenos Aires by one of its Spanish-language publishers, Gregorio Selser. Selser is a fine editor and the author of three excellent books on Nicaragua and Guatemala. The last of this trio is a full-fledged exposé of the 1954 C.I.A.-sponsored invasion to overthrow the government of popularly elected Jacobo Arbenz. Selser pushed Arévalo's book into my hands almost as soon as I stepped off the plane.

"Read it! Read it!" he told me. "Here is the key to the policies of Washington that are driving us back down the bitter road of militarism." Not long after this, the tanks rolled in Buenos Aires, in Peru, in Ecuador, in Salvador, in Brazil, as they have now rolled again in Guatemala.

Into the crazy patchwork quilt of words that concern "the noxious flower of Communism"—anti-Communism, anti-anti-Communism, anti-anti-anti-Communism, crypto-Communism, para-Communism, philo-Communism, the Communist conspiracy, fellow-traveler Communists, Trotskyites, Stalinists, Marxists, deviationists, the Red menace, Communist-front organizations, State Department Communists, and so forth—Arévalo introduces two new expressions: "Kommunism" and "anti-Kommunism." Humorously they correspond to the trend of North American advertisers to substitute "k" for "c," and are exceedingly useful. One realizes at once that they are utilized to distinguish between real Communism and fake McCarthy Communism. They serve to prick the bubbles of the ridic-

11

ulous kind of propaganda being put out in Latin America by local dictators and the enormous propaganda machine built up there by U.S. gold and bayonets. They let out some of the poison of the distortions being peddled by the American Information Service.

Arévalo begins with a simple anecdote about the murder of two innocent boys by a Guatemalan military officer, who justifies his crime by calling them "Communists." He proceeds to a devastating analysis of the operations of the police states of Latin America (that includes nearly all the countries), which are subordinate to Washington's mandates; and shows how anti-Communism (in reality anti-Kommunism) is used to maintain their nightmare rule and to try to destroy all freedom, all intellectual independence. Much of this mechanism and propaganda is directed from abroad.

He explains why the Catholic church—and he reaffirms his own Catholicism—has taken up the anti-Communist fight. He goes into the age-old philosophy of the Church, the conflicts between its creed and its institutionalized aspects. Its anti-Kommunism has far different aims than that of official U.S. policies and, in spite of its present alliance with official Washington and apparently with Protestantism, its purposes in the matter of control of the State and in education are far different. Dr. Arévalo is caustic indeed toward those high prelates in Latin America who have betrayed their trust and their doctrine to serve the interests of police-state rulers, foreign corporations, and foreign embassies rather than their own true followers.

He goes on to the "Geese of the Capitol," the big Madison Avenue boys who will stage any kind of propaganda for hire, to the big news moguls of our mass magazines and our big periodicals: the Hearsts and the Luces. The second-file geese, kept in the pens or away from the main portals, are the lesser journalists who hire out their talents to echo the official line. He presents an almost terrifying picture of monopoly of the news, of the press, of propaganda corruption, of the betrayal of freedom of the press in both North and South America.

This is a powerful, fearless book that blows away cobwebs and hypocrisies. Behind his exposition there is a deep philosophy, a far-reaching knowledge of history, economics, and sociology—an erudition that ranges over the centuries. It is a book beloved in Latin America and has circulated widely over the continent in many editions in at least three countries—even in countries where it is *Verboten*. Thanks to Lyle Stuart's edition in English, we now have a chance to share in this enlightenment and to know our neighbors better.

* * *

I first met Dr. Arévalo in the National Palace about a year after he took office; a tall, smiling, dignified personage with a curious air almost of boyish eagerness and professorial otherworldliness. He had extraordinary powers of precise logical thought and vivid verbal expression. Already he had brought to his country a new dynamic spirit of enterprise and hope. No longer did soldiers parade every block of the capital with their rifles at the ready. The only ones I saw were in the enormous barracks (the largest edifice in the city) which had been constructed along with similar ones in every hamlet in the country by Dictator Jorge Ubico, with U.S. money.

13

"Where are the soldiers?" I asked him.

"They are working the haciendas confiscated from the Germans during the war. They already produce their own food. Guatemala is too poor to afford an idle army of soldiers who gamble and get drunk in the barracks and think up depredations against the people."

Arévalo had stopped the army roundup of Indians, formerly dragged from their homes with ropes around their necks to toil on the haciendas for a few centavos a day, wages mostly pocketed by the army officers. He had established a minimum wage—at first it was thirty-five cents (which was more than twice the prevailing wage even for day laborers in the capital). Later it was raised to over a dollar a day. In this book he tells how he found farm workers in Peten working for four cents a day and how he put an end to it.

Already he had set up schools with instruction for them in their native Maya Quiché and Cachiquel languages. Magazines and newspapers were being issued and radio broadcasts given in their native tongues. And all Indians, for the first time in Guatemala's history—and they make up two-thirds of the population—were given the right to vote. That right has since been stripped away by the U.S.-imposed dictatorships, along with Arévalo's land reform, his labor reform, his new schools, and his rural clinics. He had started a crash program of housing on every hacienda in the country. That, too, was paralyzed by the C.I.A.-promoted invasion.

Already he was building highways to the coast to free the land from the United Fruit railroad monopoly, which charged more on goods from the ports to the capital than the same goods paid from any place in the world. He was

14

building a new port alongside Puerto Barrios which would be free from United Fruit control, a control of all ports obtained from previous dictatorships. For a half century that monopoly had prevented any other steamship companies of the United States or any other country from setting up regular passenger and freight service for Guatemala.

His reforms were fought tooth and nail by the U.S. Embassy; presently all aid money, so lavishly granted to Dictator Ubico, was cut off. The United Fruit Company established a maritime boycott which cut off nearly all imports, except by way of Salvador and Mexico.

The full, documented story of the aggression against Guatemala has been told in three notable books: by Guillermo Toriello, *La Batalla de Guatemala*: by Gregorio Selser, *El Guatemalazo;* and by Luís Cardoza y Aragón, *La Revolución Guatemalteca*—none of which has appeared in English. The present volume by Arévalo, continent-wide in its scope, explains why the American people have never been told the truth about Guatemala. It will explain why his mere presence in his native country to participate in an election that will not be held brought out the tanks and the gorillas. It explains why the Guatemalan people must not be free, nor those in the other banana kingdoms recently visited by President Kennedy.

—Carleton Beals

I.

A STORY
ABOUT PIGS

(Notes for a Novel about Customs)

When I arrived in Guatemala in September of 1944, called by the youth of my country to carry out the difficult assignment (in the face of a sinister government) of being the "Opposition Presidential Candidate," I had been living for the eight years previous in Argentina. Relatives, friends, leaders, and sympathizers took it upon themselves to inform me of what had occurred in Guatemala during those eight years of exile. Naturally, among the startling information supplied to me, the unusual accomplishments of the regional functionaries, military or civil, permanent or transitory, were not left out. There were materials enough to write voluminous treatises about governmental criminality.

The following is not the most macabre story but for the purposes of this book it is the most pertinent. I merely alter the names of the protagonists.

Around the year 1940, a body of the Mounted Police of the Rural Guard of Oriente and their officers halted in the city of Jutiapa [a small town about sixty miles southeast of Guatemala City on the highway to Salvador—Translator]. Their duties were to hunt down criminals—those who really were, those who were said to be, and those whom it was convenient to consider so. To hunt down crime and to practice it came to be synonymous. This Rural Guard of Oriente served equally to abuse and ruin or to maintain order. The detachment was led by Colonel Lazo, who had won his rank by serving the wishes of the bloodthirsty Señor Presidente.

While "resting" in Jutiapa, the Guard was dispersed in inns and lodging houses. For Colonel Lazo was reserved the *Comedor*, or restaurant, of Niña Filomena in one of the first houses on the road from Cuilapa. [Cuilapa is a town about thirty miles west of Jutiapa on the way to Guatemala City.—Translator] Niña Filomena, the young and good-looking owner with an extensive amorous history, was the Colonel's mistress in Jutiapa, so she enjoyed corresponding superior status in the neighborhood.

At the time of this story she was fattening two pigs especially for the New Year's celebrations when the Colonel would be back in town. The fiesta promised to be a noisy one. A marimba would play all night. (The marimba is a musical instrument with a wooden keyboard similar to that of a piano. It is never missing from Guatemalan fiestas.) There would be an abundance of tamales and an unstinting supply of liquor. There would be dancing, firecrackers, and rockets. The Señor Priest and the General, the political chief of the Department, had promised to attend. Niña Filomena, attractive and voluble, proudly showed the two pigs to all travelers. They were a special breed and though not yet six months old already measured three hand-spans high. The pigs were real personages in the locality, enjoyed full liberty, and went

18

about together through the neighborhood lots and grunted their way across pastures—even along the highway, the *camino real*.

One noon when the Colonel was waiting for his lunch, the urchin who ran errands came in complaining and tired to tell his *patrona*, Niña Filomena, that he had looked in every corner but could not find the pigs anywhere. The resultant uproar was of major proportions; nobody thought of eating. Neighbors, friends, and soldiers rushed out to search the entire neighborhood. "They passed by here," said several. "Yes, I seen them this morning," asserted another. "I swear they were the ones I came upon in the main road," insisted a man from Mita, a nearby town. But the pigs did not appear. They were given up as lost. "They have stolen Niña Filomena's piggies." "Ay, what a shame, such pretty animals." All the neighbors were sorrowful.

* * *

While the messengers of good will came and went without results, Niña Filomena wept in the Colonel's arms. At last a neighbor woman, wishing to call attention to herself and be held in esteem, approached the lovers. The García brothers were walking *by there* this morning." "*I meself seen them,*" came an echo. "Who else could have stolen them except those two big thieves?"

The García brothers were two youths not yet twenty. They had been orphans since early childhood, and lived their lives by the grace of God. Helped by most but mistreated by richer neighbors, they knew nothing of responsibilities or morals—for which they were hardly to blame. They were ready to do any kind of job, and were useful for those who asked them to work. With a habit of running

19

after girls, they were vagabondish, a bit on the bad side, but whether thieves or not the García brothers were an accepted part of that little society.

This was exactly what Colonel Lazo needed—a clue. If the pigs had been stolen—who more likely than the Garcías? He already knew these two subjects were not saints. With the rapidity of a militarist whose troops are in danger, he mobilized the men of the Guard and staked them out all over the city to find the Garcías.

Two hours later, the two boys walked, hands tied, in the midst of the mounted men. Swallowing dust and suffering blows, they were taken off to Cuilapa. Colonel Lazo had special authority granted to him by the President. He and he alone was judge, witness, government agent, and priest. In excited little groups the neighbors silently watched the troops depart. The sun was still a little high and the rifles gleamed like jewels in a cloud of golden dust.

* * *

As night began to fall over the town, the sound of mounted troops again aroused the people's curiosity. At the head of the returning band rode Colonel Lazo himself on his white-starred chestnut. The animal was bathed in sweat and spume and it champed loudly at its bit; the froth hung down on either side of its mouth like hanks of yellow cotton. Colonel Lazo dismounted by the side of the restaurant porch, tied his mount, fastened the reins to the saddle, loosened the cinch a little, slapped the animal on the rump, and entered the corridor rubbing his hands on the sleeves of his jacket with his head down. Doña Filomena was waiting. She was emotionally exhausted from her catastrophe.

20

"And my piglets?" she demanded, half sobbing.

"Lost, my dear. Those bandits refused to confess to stealing them. Then they tried to escape. You understand that the law is the law." (All such assassinations were committed under the sanction of the so-called Ley Fuga or Ley de Fuga. On passing a site selected for the purpose, prisoners were invited or obliged to run away. Some victims dropped on their knees screaming they did not want to run away, but they were killed, shot from the front or in the back. One thing was certain: the killers never neglected to put up a cross where they were buried.)

"Six men stayed behind to bury them, there in the big bend of the Cerro," the Colonel continued.

"My piglets. My piglets . . .," she cried hysterically.

Early the next morning, Colonel Lazo dictated his report for his superiors to an old experienced clerk in the *Jefatura Política,* who understood law and had good handwriting.

Two boys burst into the house, shouting, "Ña Filo! Ña Filo! We found your piggies."

"Over yonder in the gully, going toward the irrigation ditch."

They got their breath back, and one added: "Looks as if they're trapped and can't get out."

The beautiful Niña Filo and the handsome Colonel, his moustaches like horns with waxed upturned ends, looked intently into each other's eyes for a moment, scarcely breathing. Then the Colonel resumed cleaning his nails with a little knife and, without looking at her, replied to her tacit question:

"Don't be upset, my darling. The García brothers were Communists."

II.

THE POLICE RULERS AND THEIR ANTI-KOMMUNISM

We are here to prevent the enemy from trapping the standard-bearer, or the flag from falling into the wrong hands.

—José Martí (the father of the first Cuban Independence)

This is not a fight to the death against what is usually called Communism, but an implacable attack on liberty.

—Vicente Sáenz (a prolific Costa Rican writer and university professor, who has led a lifelong crusade against imperialism in the Americas, particularly in Central America)

This book begins with elementary sociological assumptions, not yet proved, which will serve as a plausible working hypothesis to explain our position and strip bare the comedy being played right now in the halls of government, in the courts of justice, at international conferences; and thereby to penetrate the drama of our peoples in the intimacy of their homes, in the gatherings of youth, in the interior of factories, in the depths of mines, in the open air and the strong light of the fields.

Immediately we are confronted with antagonistic strata of our national life: the powerful minority of those who rule; the non-participating majority of those ruled. These are two opposite worlds, each day further apart, each day more hostile. This phenomenon of growing alienation corresponds to a subjective process, not on the sociological level, but originating in psychology and morality, its philosophical roots decidedly instinctive. These areas, which we term subjective, are formed by the congealing of unequal irreconcilable interests.

Material interests produce in each of our countries a predetermined political current, expressed in economic activities, in commercial practices, in actual political aspirations, until they finally become a theory of the State, or sometimes a theory negating the State. In contrast, the popular layers of the population, which do not conceive of commerce as being life's basic purpose, are oriented in political currents incompatible with the former; they subordinate economic factors to other vital values among which they give a leading role to the dignity of the individual and his fight for liberty. In the abstract, they conceive of justice as very noble and not limited to wage increases, and they aspire to political participation, and thus arrive at their own theory of government.

The Latin American peoples (I don't know if this occurs also in European societies) carry on public controversy on the basis of these two above-mentioned currents. On the one hand, there is the powerful minority, barricaded by its ramified interests and defended by a police

23

apparatus, paid for by the money of all citizens; on the other, the great majority who have no millions to protect, who instinctively struggle for minimum material goods and for maximum moral goals, and are preoccupied fundamentally with the education of their children and with meaningful existence. From the struggle between these two ways of evaluating life arise the obvious and contradictory aspects we call public life.

Two forms of government predominate in Latin America as the visible outgrowth of that intimate struggle. On the one hand, the Police Rulers, installed in power to maintain intact the laws which perpetuate systems of exploitation; and Representative Leaders, who try to modify those laws to give the masses a breathing space and elevate them to more human levels of life. Every revolutionary movement in Latin America always results in an individual or collective representative government—whether or not it is composed of army representatives. All too fleeting are the moments in which the people try to make themselves heard and produce this type of government. The masses do not always have luck enough to choose their representatives well; in most instances the men to whom the people give their confidence succumb to the temptations that surround them or simply join the brotherhood of the millionaires and, as by magic, power falls again into the hands of the old ruling clique without any need for new elections.

This explains why the majority of governments are police states and last longer. But it would be unjust to say that the people in Latin America have a "talent" for police rule. There is a permanent game of chance in which tricksters pull away the leaders of the masses; the spokesman for the plebes turns into another gendarme; the Liberator becomes the hangman or the instrument of hangmen. It's a game of chance in which the good and the evil qualities that exist in every human being are made use of in varying degrees. It is a psychological contest which results in a certain strengthening of nerves and muscles which form the monstrous mandibular mechanism of the few, at the cost of the vital minimum of existence for the many, and which corrupts the essence that is man. Thus those elected by the majority to break through the unethical legal crust end up, as if by magic, being themselves transformed into crust. A tragic process of petrification known in politics as betrayal!

*　　*　　*

Having sketched our hypothesis, let us proceed to examine a Police Ruler—any one at all. The Police Ruler does not govern, he administers. He is the great administrator of vast properties—of the property of others at the beginning—which in the end belong to him and his group. These goods are called "the interests of the nation." This is not the truth. The interests of the nation are quite different. What these rulers protect and administer are the interests of a minority, of a social nucleus dedicated to big business: a certain number of traditional and parvenu families who require a police force always larger, always stronger. And this police force does not stop growing until it becomes the government itself. Governments then function from top to bottom as a perfect police organization.

It is not essential that a Police Ruler be a soldier. When

a civilian becomes the Police Ruler, he is usually more primitive and more brutal than the notorious Army Colonels. This type of ruler provided the picturesque note in our America in the last century, and was immortalized in the person of the brutal Ecuadorean Veintemilla, thanks to the pen of the great critic Juan Montalvo.

[General Ignacio Veintemilla was a Conservative turn-coat who seized power in Ecuador in 1876 in the name of the Radical Liberal Party. Of his regime Antonio Barrera, the deposed constitutionally elected President who was long imprisoned and finally sent into exile, wrote: "A gang of hungry bandits, thirsting for vengeance, who have seized the destinies of the country and the public moneys, with no other aim than to live according to the laws of Epicurus."

[Juan Montalvo, often called Ecuador's greatest nineteenth-century writer, was a fine terse stylist, a liberal in politics, a mordantly satirical anti-clerical, a consistent enemy of dictators and oppression. He vividly described the manner in which Veintemilla, on fleeing the country, looted the banks of Guayaquil.—Translator]

At the beginning of our century the species reappears; but instead of a Montalvo there steps forward a Vallenilla Lanz who praised and justified them as "the only force for conserving society."[1] [Vallenilla, a prolific newspaper and book writer, was the head of the Venezuelan Senate under the bloody Vicente Gómez, perhaps the worst tyrant in the history of the Americas, who gave away his country to Standard Oil. Vallenilla was his chief intellectual hireling and apologist, though in the United States Gómez enjoyed an even greater body of intellectual and official eulogists who exalted his "progress" to the skies, but neglected to mention Venezuela's poverty, misery, and political blood baths.—Translator]

On the eve of World War II, Latin America offered the same picturesque spectacle and suffered from a goodly proportion of Police Rulers, *totalitarian style,* whose aid was solicited, even so, to "defend democracy" against the Nazism of those days. After the war was over, the United States found pretexts for continuing to utilize this kind of "foreign" servants, who so solicitously care for the interests of the minority of their fellow countrymen. From the long secular experience of Great Britain, we know already that such minorities, enjoying economic advantages, are the best allies when the hour of imperialistic penetration arrives. In India "a powerful group of wealthy landholders had a strong interest in the continuation of British domination, under which they completely dominated the mass of the people." This was stated by Lord Bentick, the Governor General, in 1829.[2] This explains why England needed only one Englishman to rule every two thousand Asiatics. Now the main characteristics of a new interpolated imperialism have been established in the Occidental World—the Police Rulers together with their national oligarchies have come to be the guardians of the interests of the Empire, i.e., of the interests of a minority who govern the Occident from New York.

*　*　*

At the same time, the Latin Americans, a little tired, ashamed perhaps of so much police, penitentiary, and colonial humiliation have not sold out and continue to nurse the hope of being governed by statesmen. For statesmen they *did* have during the previous century: men trained in the study of law, of social philosophy, economics, diplomacy, and political history. An admirable criterion prevailed. Nowadays something more is needed than erudition and polished manners to play the role of this rare type of representative, whom the people ask for insistently for their own good health. More than the illustrious virtues of polished education and scholarship, the men which the Latin American peoples ask for, and insist on having, must display elementary psychological virtues, especially those which have to do with *hormones.* Changed political conditions have shoved aside the intellectual in favor of the biological specimen, and the leader must have claws apt for fighting—the he-man, every inch the he-man.

The shift in political power from local governments to the Empire, the incessant propaganda discrediting the concept of sovereignty, the imposition of treaties and covenants because of the real or fancied need for loans, the big press's intimidation of any government which tries to defend any other point of view, the hidden but ever-constant threat of ambassadors, who fabricate revolutions or dollar droughts when presidents don't come across—all this has come to replace the merit of what was once considered the true mission of a statesman. Now the ruler must have more primitive drive, he-man energies, which shamefully our sex-leveling civilization makes scarcer night by night. When we were sovereign Republics, the statesman satisfied popular aspirations, and the *head,* the command in each country, was really in the Palace of government. But now, mid-century having gone by, the statesman is not enough, because the ruler has to solve, so to speak, the *problem of frontiers,* the problem of outsiders intrud-

28

ing into the house, outsiders who try to rule us. Diplomacy along French traditions and erudition are no longer enough to defend us. A popular government in this hour of house-cleaning requires, in addition to the symbolic broom, the domestic cudgel of our grandfathers.

There was a good deal of sense in the old figure of speech which compared ruling *to steering a ship,* in which the pilot is the only person responsible for the voyage; his duty, to guide it in such a way that it always stays on its course and always reaches its destination with safety, without mishaps, through storm and dangerous shoals, with care for crew and passengers. Everyone was conscious of the image of the Pilot-leader; he was the *Statesman Pilot.*

But in this hour of tremendous danger on the high seas, the ship's pilot is no longer the real pilot: our ruler is not our pilot. Our ships are guided by remote control—by radar. Our fellow countryman only seems to be the pilot. The Pilot-in-Chief is to be found in the Pilot-Ship, the Flagship. If there is to be a storm—from which direction the winds blow, whether we should or should not unfurl our sails or break out the oars, whether the cargo is excessive and the ship becalmed, whether we ought to take off our clothes or throw the coffee overboard, whether tonight or at daybreak—all this is transmitted to us from outside. For this, statesmen are not needed. All we need are Police Rulers, perfect administrators, enforcers of order, those who manufacture silence with the scream of bullets. The *Fascist theory* of "letting the chief think for us," this is no longer domestic theory in a state; it is now the colonial mentality of states which recognize the Metropole's right to think for them and thus save them that wearisome and dangerous task.

The government of *each province* is reduced to simple terms and very comfortable functions: to look after privileges and laws, follow out foreign instructions which perpetuate them in office, keep the natives peaceful, watch all ports of entry, send out products faithfully and at a good price, buy tons of showy glass beads. For this what is better than a Police Ruler? Why any need for statesmen? The Police Rulers wallow in the pleasures of sensual enjoyment which drug them into complacent obedience. The Police Rulers know how to give orders, and like to do so; they know how to obey, and that pleases them too. They give orders to their compatriots; they *obey the Empire*. And when there are demonstrations in the streets, they put them down with machine-guns. (It has become the norm for Police Rulers to disperse street demonstrations by students, still in their teens, by rifle and machine-gun fire. Thus far not a single Latin American government has dared denounce such crimes before the Organization of American States or the United Nations. The League of Governments carries on fraternally.)

Because the Empire needs peace within its frontiers, there is not even a buzz of flies that might interfere with the ability to locate the flight of an enemy plane a thousand kilometers high. The truth is that Latin America, a zone "occupied" by *treaties* and pacts subscribed to *"in perpetuity"* is no longer a problem. The Empire is interested in more distant places, markets and military bases beyond the Atlantic, beyond the Pacific, to the North and to the South as far as the Poles. This Happy Arcadia, "well-governed," requires little effort; there is scarcely a whisper of our economic problems, expounded by us with the air of obsequious hangers-on. To the extent that when we

30

assembled in Buenos Aires for the August, 1957, Economic Conference to "discuss," the only thing we did with any courage was . . . beg and beg . . . and beg. . . . Beg and insist on more and more *dollars*. And the Empire, cruel, very cruel, merely told us that it could give us no more. . . . An English journalist of the *Times* said of us in those shameful days that we gave the impression of animals fighting over their feed.[3] What a strong figure of speech! But even stronger, and sans metaphor, are documents and facts; weeks later proud Albion [Britain] needed dollars and the United States rushed over five hundred millions. But let's not think about that feed-crib called the Marshall Plan.

It would be insulting to say that we have an aptitude for the feed-crib. The materialism of our epoch has not yet reached that point. But the truth is, the brilliant French philosopher's formula "I think, therefore I exist," by which he assuaged his speculative anguish has become *"I exist for my feed,"* the anguish of Latin America at this hour. And he who exists for his feed must obey the orders of the monopolist who accumulates and administers the feed. But if we do not have an "aptitude for the feed crib," we certainly do have a talent for sensual living, a talent for animal satisfactions, a talent for elementary life without problems, without metaphysics, without any philosophy of law or of wrong-doing . . . which serves to mitigate the pain of falling into a protectorate state, whether the people wish it or not.

Is there not some juridical fiction abroad which says: if the Government wishes something it is because the Nation wishes it? Pan-American jurists assure us that when a Police Ruler signs an agreement he is interpreting the

31

true sentiments of his people. And just try, by shouting in the middle of the street, to undo that knot, tied "in perpetuity"—for all time—by a Police Ruler in "conformity with the law."

* * *

The same juridical fiction serves to convert Republics into Colonies: any head of state can mortgage forever the *property of his country*; it encourages Police Rulers to set up as their private domain other fictitious legalisms which give crime the aspect of virtue. We have just seen how Colonel Lazo of Jutiapa justified two killings with a convenient word. Having murdered the García brothers, he prepared a report to his superiors, mentioning several articles of the penal code, took the testimony of nonexistent witnesses, and justice was thereby satisfied. Killing two men in the flower of life for the crime of being Kommunists constitutes a juridical sign of the new times, inspired in the same fiction by which a de facto government can play dice with the properties of the nation. If the Empire claims immunity for its "public service" enterprises, then the same immunity extends also to enterprises of "public order" carried on by the same primitive ruler.

For centuries on centuries, it has been a crime, a very grave crime, to steal. To this class of crimes, however, belong only those seen from-above-looking-down. The robberies of a millionaire, who steals from habit, and the robberies by the ruler, who steals for sport, are not punishable and are not punished. (Evidently I am not the only one who looks at the matter in this way. The Experimental Theater of Chile, an official cultural institution, in presenting "Thieves' Carnival," by Jean Anouilh in October and November, 1957, presented an explanation in the program, one paragraph of which states: "two new friends, the Señores Dupont Dufort—father and son—two respectable thieves, that is, two financiers.")

Who would ever think of denouncing a millionaire for continuing to steal? Who but a mad man can believe that a policeman, the model for all patriots, is using the government to fill his own saddlebags? Optical illusions— say the lawyers, and the judges, and the big newspapers. But let a simple man on the street make the same mistake, and the lawyer will accuse him, the judge will put him in jail, the press will bewail his act as a sickness eating away the foundations of social morality.

The sentence of death has just been meted out to an unhappy Negro in Alabama because he stole under the cover of night, one dollar and ninety-five cents.[4] Four others, also Negroes, died before he did, also in Alabama, because they too stole at night. Theft must be done by the light of day, a Rockefeller would say, and one should not be such an imbecile as to steal only pennies.

A thief is one who steals bread for his children, or a jacket to cover himself, or medicine to cure himself. Jean Valjean, Victor Hugo's thief! He who exploits a conglomeration of fellow-citizens without quarter or pity to amass a fortune which not even his descendants will consume in a hundred years is a patriot; he shows a spirit of enterprise. The García brothers of Jutiapa: these are the thieves for whose crimes the laws and justice are concerned. Colonel Lazo killed them to keep on good terms with his mistress; he alone decided; and his exploit was recognized by a promotion or by a salary increase or by a decoration. The notion of crime, the notion of justice, the notion of

33

law itself have fundamentally changed in the middle of this century.

* * *

"Don't be upset, my precious, the García brothers were Kommunists." Here you have the Police State governor, creator of law, protector of society, firm right arm of justice. Because Colonel Lazo is a governor. To be such it is not absolutely necessary to occupy the highest office of public administration. Many there do not even govern. Has not Disraeli already said it about monarchs? He governs who acts, who executes, who gives orders, whatever his position. The Police Rulers are prepared—gain their experience—at the bottom and even now are preparing themselves to "deserve" future high position. As governors, they are apprentices; but as policemen they are past masters. They are the magicians of order, of public security. They are prepared for the future in the fetid waters of the present. They accumulate in their record episodes like that of the story of the pigs. They persecute Kommunism, the universal social calamity. And when they are fixing a cross over the ditch even before it is completely filled, the blood stains still visible, they look tranquilly toward the Empire and wink.

* * *

The government which desires to enjoy access to the feed-crib—spoken of by our English detractor and competitor—must be anti-Kommunist. It does not matter what political ideas the people who arrive in the administration may have; the important thing is that "the Government," that is to say, the police, follow the imperialist line of *persecuting Kommunism,* as it is understood by the Yankees, in the form it is understood by the Catholic

34

Church, and in the form it is understood by the police themselves. To speak truthfully, the Gendarmes are professionally disposed to combat Kommunism. They have been given—they have always been given—an ingrown predisposition to predicate and practice anti-Kommunism. It is what Darwin considered (in animals) a "prophetic" trait—manisfestations that anticipate the evolution of the species, what is known as . . . involution. Since the word "Kommunism" has been batted about as a confused symbol of agitation, perturbation, reformism, democracy, and progress—a word blown up by the rancor of the French monarchs, the Russian Tsarists, the Kaiser's Prussians (and by the millionaires of New York)—the police-state rulers have astutely seized upon the potentialities of the new word for domestic purposes. It is to them we owe the early adaptation of the magic word to our provincial life— much before the continental Metropole used it to serve a philosophy of imperialism.

In my first message as a presidential candidate,[5] I affirmed that Nazism and fascism were merely hothouse plants carried to Europe from their natural nursery: Latin America. I repeated this when in the presidency. This empirical Nazism of Central America and South America was intrinsic with our Police-State rulers, ideologically and in practice. Hitler and Mussolini dressed it up in modern clothes and injected philosophy into it. But anti-Kommunism, as a police activity, as a pretext for destroying street demonstrations and for the penitentiary policy, existed previously in Latin America. Naturally, with more sincerity and high-handedness in the Caribbean.

At the present time, anti-Kommunism is an international slogan created by the merging of various currents, foreign to each other. These trends have no homogeneity. The most diverse people propagate the slogan. Temporary expediences even promote it. More than a doctrine, more than a political theory, it wears the garb of a practical tool: a wall to block off the wide avenue of popular revindications; a barricade to hold back social progress, the rights of the humble, a just distribution of wealth, and the winning of national control by the people. It is not the result of any logical inquiry. Better said, it is the taking advantage of a certain psychological irritation, vengeful and *revanchista*, which is converted quickly into an order given to the enemies of the people—a realistic, very useful order. The Police-State Gendarmes, who carry out orders, enjoy thereby important personal benefits. The same thing happens with the merchants of New York, with the Holy Mother Catholic Church, with the entrepreneurs of the major press, and all the social climbers. Anti-Kommunism serves them all and it serves for every sort of advantage, but chiefly to clear the road for predatory gain and to close off the other road; that of liberating the popular majorities.

* * *

Already we know that every thief is a Kommunist, the ingenuous excuse of the real criminal whom we met in the Introduction. We cannot argue that any Colonel Lazo has ever examined the historic meaning of property or the legal network that has protected it since the beginning of Empire. Stealing, petty thievery, the Colonel would say, is the occupation of lazy bums.[6] The life of society, as understood by the Gendarme, is action, work, trail-making, accomplishment, the harvest, productivity at so much percent profit. The history of rapine does not awaken his mental curiosity. Logic and history have always been the concern of idle pedants unable to do a daily job. Life is the road, the march, the planting. Colonel Lazo would say that this road is on foot for the humble, forced marches for the adversary, and the sowing of crosses because of the multiplying of graves. But this is mere talk; what is real is that *life is the highway, the marches, the harvesting.* For these reasons—or for no reason at all—the Guatemalan colonel justified to his own simple-minded conscience that all assassinations which "justice" recommended to him and those which, due to de facto circumstances, he perpetuated on his own initiative, were a proper fulfillment of justice, i.e., the justice as determined by the Señor Presidente.

To *kill* certain thieves, regardless of what was stolen, whatever its price or value, in Guatemala (as in Alabama) is the function of good government. It is not a question of logic or political philosophy; it is simply imperialistic tradition. In short, the Government, in Republican states, carries on its back a never-examined form of social punishment. At first it would seem to be a concern of people without profession or money. A certain number of citizens keep watch from their homes on the actions of the government and tolerate its acts so long as they do not affect the fundamental interests of *their* group. These are the four families of imperial Japan. They are the three hundred families of great Germany. They are the thousand North Americans of the Empire. Here among us there are the big landholders, the businessmen, the importers and exporters. The destinies of the country and the destinies of their own properties are identified. This government, or any other, can be tolerated so long as they prosper. There is no conscience about public affairs, the nation, the fatherland. A government which interests itself for the whole, which talks of "popular majorities," which legislates for others, is doomed. A sordid confabulation of powerful interests crowds it to the wall, with big newspapers leading the pack. Private property is in danger! Sacred private property!

"Private property is theft," cried Proudhon in 1840. But "from sad necessity, the laws awarded the rich what they had usurped,"[7] a French sacerdote confessed, beating his breast in the pulpit before his congregation. Thus property acquired by usurpation came to be a religious institution. Sacred Property! The merchants and priests, allied in this fashion, soon sought participation in government and governmental protection, so private property became also a political institution.[8] Merchants, priests, and rulers of government thereby determined automatically the social character of the thief, the Kommunist in the streets, as endangering the most powerful social institution. Government, previously despicable, the refuge of people lacking a profession, became something important with a mission of salvation, the protection of all things sacred. In Latin America this sanctification of property is more recent.

The native countries were subjugated by force, cheated according to law, soothed and put to sleep by the clergy. What had once been the right of the owners of the country came to be the right of the Conquistadores, who arrived with Cross and all. Brute force brought to this continent the European concept of property. They brought us Roman law with its imperial fanfare. With the sword, the line was drawn: here and no farther, and with dagger in hand the natives were told "Shut up!" The symbolic Cross presided over this ceremony in the plaza. The mayor and notaries fabricated documents which were duly filed in the archives. On the heels of the priest and the notary came the loan-merchants to "aid" the dispossessed Indian. Mediterranean usury (Phoenician, Carthaginian, Genovesian, Venetian) was the stew that incubated our nationalities, and this still continues to be the sustenance of the elite, the *gentes de bien*.

Thus we live in a tangle of lies, fabricated by criminals. No crime exists that has not been disguised as virtue. And it is with these "virtues" we are obliged to exist. Colonel Lazo knew it by instinct. He was no fool. What follows are the professors discussing and the statesman making "plans." His nose, his instinct, tells him that if he kills to protect "sacred property," he will have a lawyer; he *will have a priest* all the way to heaven. The prototype is Royalist rule, deeds originally written with the sword, as Spencer said. Colonel Lazo fabricates with his rifles the greatest possible number of repetitions of the original evil deeds. And his authority is so great he can make use of the Cross itself and plant it there where the Kommunist is buried.

"The proprietors of rural fincas which are fenced in, or their legitimate representatives, *will be exempt from criminal responsibility* for any crimes they commit against unauthorized individuals who, having penetrated inside the property, are discovered in flagrant seizing or carrying off animals, fruit, products, or tools belonging to the same."—Legislative decree 2795, promulgated April 27, 1944, by the Police Ruler of Guatemala, General Jorge Ubico.

In other words, kill whoever robs, be it a theft of a

39

broom or a hammer. Property is sacred. The fincas are feudal domains. Assassination is a virtue. This is Guatemala, country of the Caribbean. But let us go far south. Near Santiago de Chile, on March 28, 1957, a thirty-year-old man, Manuel Méndez Bernal, was killed by a rifle shot when he was surprised taking some ears of corn.[9] The property is owned by the Salesian Fathers, and the corn therefore was the sacred property of the curates. The Winchester was fired by a holy man, Reverend Ramiro Tejido Parra, principal of the Agrarian School. This minister of Christ, like any other Police-State ruler, understands quite well that one can take a life for an ear of corn. "Don't be upset, Precious, the García brothers were Kommunists." Isn't it so, Reverend Father?

Thus it is quite evident that the simple-mindedness of confusing thieves with Communists is not restricted to the murky conscience of a Colonel Lazo. We have just seen that the learned consciences of pedagogical priests also level themselves down to this same simple-mindedness. The brothers García, two vagabond boys, lived well or badly at this banquet of properties they did not own by sneaking about in order to survive. To sneak about pilfering is an animal custom. We notice that men too have the temptation to return to the past existence of our species. Culture and pride prevent our obeying the impulse; therefore, if a man goes about pilfering what is not his, this should not upset his competitors so much. Is not universal history a history of roaming about and robbing? Was it not a roaming and a robbery by the sixteenth-century Spaniards of a whole continent that did not belong to them? And do not the Yankees go roaming and robbing on

40

the four continents of the earth now in this twentieth
century?

* * *

The García brothers lived any way they could. They
did not even know if they had been born of the same
father. Their neighbors went to school, but the pangs of
hunger did not permit them to learn to read. They had
no property because the banquet table was already full,
and they were not old enough to learn the *morals of self-
enrichment.* The plebeian thieves always remain poor.
They could not even become stockholders, the latest sacred
system; they were like antisocial cysts. They consumed
without producing. They robbed without even having the
excuse of being "men of business" or "knights of industry."
They cut the fruit of the orchard that was not theirs. They
were thieves of the people, vulgar parasites, not adapted as
yet to the elegant ways of thievery, *the legal ways to steal.*
But they were likeable boys. No one hated them, because
they never killed in order to steal, nor did they hide out
after taking something, nor did they ever steal anything
at all valuable. They knew how to be useful at certain
times: they went on errands even to other towns, they took
care of herds of cattle, accompanied respectable Señoras
on dangerous trips, and how many times—life is indeed
enigmatic—they were left to guard a vacant house, proud
to take care of it. They lived by gifts, by tips, by popular
affection, little gifts, little tips. Never any large gift or any
really huge tips. None of the great gifts, the enormous tips
handed out, for example, by the United Fruit to the
Caribbean Presidents. The García brothers moved in other
circles and had a different set of morals. Village society

41

sympathized with them because they were the bottomless well of its own conscience; everybody knew that the García brothers were a social "fact," a legitimate product of the society that surrounded them.

Children without parents, children without schooling, how many are there? And men who go about pilfering the property of others, how many are there? Are you unaware, Reader, that Police-State governors seize property not theirs? Don't you know how the fortune of General Trujillo of Santo Domingo began and how it grew—that great moralist and anti-Kommunist?[10] Roaming about and stealing, thievery and robbery, are not the exclusive monopoly of orphans and illiterates.

The awareness of Colonel Lazo did not even go this far. For him the García brothers were "thieves" and property is "sacred." *Human life is not.* But let us not quarrel with him too much. He is carrying out the duties of his position. As agent of the government, he represents "authority." He receives orders concerning justice, and when he does not receive any, he imagines what they are and obeys his own orders. He has heard that justice, in turn, receives orders, and that the President of the country also receives orders, but this is not a matter of his concern.

That every thief is a Kommunist is axiomatic for men like Colonel Lazo. The gendarmes, the police—at least those in the Caribbean—admit that this is the case. It is an axiom of government, of good government. Killing thieves provides a justification for *being in power.* In the Caribbean, at any event, "To govern is to kill." Robbery is an assault against the most important social institution. Killing is not. *Because human life is not a social institution.* The more persons killed, the stronger is the regime. The

42

solid stability of these Caribbean governments is clotted with blood, the blood of cheap thieves, the sneak thieves, thieves without public office, thieves without medals and decorations.

We are accustomed to be unjust in our appreciation of these Caribbean rulers who earn their existence so wearisomely amid slime, dirt, and blood. Their cultural limitations permit us to make jokes or write caustic pages. The truth is something else. The elemental confusion between thief and Kommunist has had antecedents or it comes from orders from spheres of higher culture. The story is told, for example, that when the English and Yankee imperialists enjoyed the profits created by *Russian oil*, with the title of "owners," the press, twice as imperialistic, was benevolent toward the "revolutionary experiments" of the Bolsheviks. It merely required that the Russians "nationalize" their oil for their government to become at once a regime of reprobates and for Communists to be universally labeled thieves.[11]

The Mexican governments were called Kommunists already by 1926, when the regime of Plutarco Elías Calles nationalized the subsoil; but this Kommunism was raised to the category of "thieves" when President Cárdenas simplified the matter by declaring that oil was Mexican and what was Mexican was Mexican.[12] Kommunists and thieves were the Argentines also during one period of their history; when President Perón nationalized the railroads and the meat plants. The epithets naturally came from England, which believed itself the owner of those services and of that country. But the British went even further; according to them besides being thieves and Kommunists, the Argentines were also *"traitors."* The *Daily Express*, April,

1957, spoke of "the railroads, British property, stolen by Perón." With the news of loans of money by England to the Argentine government of Aramburu, the paper said, "The brothers of British blood, brothers within the Commonwealth (referring to Australia), are left to one side in favor of foreigners with a record of being traitors." [Translated from the Spanish.] [13]

* * *

I have brought these documents out of my files in defense of Colonel Lazo. For the kinship between poor thief and Kommunist has *European antecedents* and is not an exclusive contrivance of the Police Rulers. Here, as over there, the police have been transformed into the basic instrument for fighting what is believed to be Kommunism! That is, the thievery of the poor, which is very similar to the petty thievery of *weak nations*. The police take good care not to try to control the pecuniary customs of persons of other hierarchies. Because the truth is, there are footpads who are Kommunists and footpads who are not: thieves who are thieves, and thieves who are not. And there are persons who play with the idea in a sensational way, shouting in the middle of the street what you would like to hear expressed by other lips. For example:

"Bolshevism hammers at our doors. We cannot allow it to enter. We must organize against it; stand together shoulder to shoulder and hold firm. We must keep our America intact, save it from destruction. We must protect the workers against Red propaganda, against Red trickery, and make sure that their spirit remains healthy."

A Protestant preacher? A Catholic prelate? No, these words were said by an honorable Yankee, a moralist and anti-Kommunist to the core. They are the words of *Al Capone*.[14] He uttered them in 1931—by an irritating coincidence the same year in which assumed power a Police Ruler, Jorge Ubico, anti-Kommunist like Al Capone and, like Al Capone, author of a *Law of Probity*, which forbade public officials (that is, the underlings) to enrich themselves, while his own fortune multiplied fabulously in spite of the law. It is the same Police Ruler who ordered that anybody who stole five dollars be shot, but had the Legislative Assembly make him a gift of two hundred thousand dollars. He is the superior of Colonel Lazo, whom we saw shoot two men suspected of stealing two pigs. We are therefore now living under a new moral law, under new codes, under different skies. Those of us who harbor a certain undefined criterion of delinquency should learn the contemporary variations.

*   *   *

Nothing is easier than to lose oneself when traveling inside the mental fog of the Police Rulers. But their concept of law is the best guiding thread by which to move forward. Their defense of social institutions is also a clear guide. Let us proceed, therefore, from those delinquents of low origin, called thieves, to consider the slightly superior delinquents called "agitators." Social agitators, to be more precise.

The social institutions provide the pretext: to hang on to power is the real reason. The Police Rulers, like the guards of a religious temple, know little or nothing of what is inside or what the altars, the rites, the symbols signify. They are merely guarding the properties of others for hire. Be it a temple of the true believer or of an an-

tagonistic sect, of believers of their own faith or of heterodox reprobates, whatever they protect is all the same for
them. They are guards, this they can understand. Alas for
anyone who comes to the doors of the temple at night!
Alas for anyone who walks over the carpets with bare feet!

"Social agitators" belong to a line of individuals without
lineage, individuals whose existence is inexplicable to the
Police Rulers. They are persons who preach exotic doctrines in the streets, who use imported words, who talk
about a new society, who urge changes in customs, who
ask for a better life, who describe terrestrial paradises, but
at the same time give bad advice, denounce wrongs, and
expose the crimes of the police, point their fingers at the
guilty; they invite disobedience, they protest, threaten,
and prepare the road for rebellions. They are the reprobates without caste, the disinherited, the Godless men
without a country.

We are thinking about Jesus Christ, who, for Police
Ruler Herod Antipas had neither country nor God. He
was the prototype of the "social agitator," discontented,
rebellious, heterodox, who spoke of a better life and other
gods.[15] His symbolic crucifixion between two vulgar
thieves, Kommunists like him, calls for no further explanations. And we would be considered stupidly insulting
were we to speak of Socrates as a second example of the
"social agitator" whom the police persecuted. Socrates,
like Jesus, stimulated people to think about a new life,
about other Gods, and he led Youth along roads which had
nothing to do with the "social institutions" of his epoch.
Those rulers killed him. Now 2,400 years later, he still
lives.

Like these, very much like them, are the "social agitators" of today, except that it would be impossible to demand that everyone have a new religion or a new philosophy. Without being a religion or a philosophy, syndicalism (the labor unions) has had the quality of bringing down on itself the wrath of the police and the judges. As old as Socrates and Jesus, labor movements reappear from time to time, possibly in differing forms. Yet the millionaires of the world were always unionized: money is a powerful cement; the religions are also unions; faith is cement for the multitude; a more powerful union than that of the militarists one cannot ask for; Masonry is a great union; political parties are unions. The Organization of American States is the most modern of these unions; it is a union of governments which have found the way to defend themselves against those ruled.

When a whole people rise up, as they did in Cuba, the Organization of American States looks the other way; and Police Rule, among the rest at least, is saved. Another union is the North Atlantic Alliance. This is the union of industrialists who manufacture arms; and it must always be able to count on governments to buy them, whether the arms are needed or not. But the unionization of workers who wish to defend their wages: this cannot be permitted. Or if it is permitted, they must be spied upon, listened in upon, registered, interrogated, jailed. It is a unionism of the unfortunate. It is not the unionism of the Powerful. Unionism among the humble is like a curse that is watched, or a contagious malady, or a torrent that bursts out, or a fire that devours. "Social cancer," nothing more, nothing less. The Police Rulers feel a definite personal hostility toward such unions. It is the same animosity they have for petty thieves. It is not that they

47

understand unionism; simply that they hate it, and that hate prevents them from understanding it. They suspect that unionism limits their authority; they look upon the spokesman for the unions as a competitor; and they fight him blindly, with clenched fists, with kicks and bites, or with machine guns. The same machine guns that are paid for by the sweat and health of the workers!

In the Caribbean, the quarrel has been zoological, bestial. The lower the standard of living, the loftier is the point of view, the deeper the animosity. The worse the sickness inside the body, the greater the lust to die by killing. Never have rebellions been as bloody as when the people fight for the elementary biological survival of their children. In the Caribbean, the contradictory meaning of what is human—they say—is that life, like honor, is defended by dying, but dying by fighting to punish the betrayers of human life—those who kill two men for two pigs, those who murder a man because he stole a dollar. And those who fight this battle, even before they begin, renounce hospitals, doctors, and elaborate funerals they do not enjoy and never will enjoy.

Thus among us in the Caribbean, labor unionism is mixed up with nonlabor elements, with the civic ferment, with political waves so great they seem to be a new struggle for independence. If the Police Rulers have delivered the country to the foreigner, the organized people can recover it. For the masses, when they unite, do not do so merely to defend themselves from their fellow countrymen who traffic with the national goods, but the foreign merchant who sells his merchandise in the office of the president itself. They fight against the foreign flags which wave, visible or invisible, at the top of the flag poles over our

48

Palaces of Government. Looter of the public treasuries, the Police Ruler is also the guardian for imperialistic interests. There lies the secret of our downfall as Republics.

It is fruitful and amusing to analyze the patriotic sentiment of the Police Rulers. But let us not get over-tragic about it. All empires have always recognized the double nationality of the conquered, the subjugated, the colonies, the barbarians. But it is the same citizenship whatever the nationality. The empires know enough to appreciate this duality within the imperial unity. Patriotism is steadily transferred toward the Metropole. Foreign interests and native interests find in the Police Ruler the prototype of the patriots of the Empire.

But not merely in the Caribbean and thereabouts, certainly, has the union of the humble been heretical and the concern of "reprobates." The social institutions endangered by unionism—the aristocratic and bourgeois way of life, of squeezing out the juice and storing it up—of playful enjoyment and playful profit—that juicy profitable existence and that profitable play of days on end, of months and years, were no Caribbean invention. It's the brief colorful history that has had its London, its Berlin, its Hamburg and its Florence, and who knows but also its Rome and Carthage: its Sodom and Gomorrah! According to Renan, the poor in the Roman Empire were denied even the simple right of assembly or associating. They had to live in isolation unable to share their miseries.[16]

But here in our America there is a new and diverse society; here our Latin countries are naturally cruder, more elementary, without feudal castles or drawbridges, without thousand-year-old traditions, without sacred

49

parchments, without perfection in the vices, lacking what is exquisite and refined, lacking social class barriers. It is here that institutions—that is to say what is sacred—are closer at hand to the plebes, and the plebes are less inhibited, and recognize no mental obstacles or prejudices; the rulers have been easier to get at in hours of rebellion and punishment. That is why the collision of social forces has been easier and more frequent, without class consciousness or class hate, with little meaning except the conscious effort to survive and without hate except that produced by obstacles to that desire to live. That is why here "social agitators" seem larger than mountains in the imagination of the petty criminal palace ruler.

If the gods had had a little more pity, they would have enlightened the Police Rulers of another possibility: that the "social agitators" are the best assistants imaginable in pointing out and solving problems of government. But no. The gods, close-mouthed as always, offered no light and hence have provided a great deal of artificial might to the social coercion of the people in the form of ostentatious and trigger-happy guards and torturers. It is social retrogression, to be sure. For always, from primitive Rome until pre-revolutionary Europe, it was always a function of government to protect the humble against the bad habits of the powerful, to protect the poor against the rapacity of the rich, to protect those unable to buy arms for private use against those who could. All the egoism and cruelty of the oligarchies, medieval or modern, found in royalty a check, a vigilante, a judge. *To Govern is to Protect.* "Down with the rich! Long live the Emperor!" the French peasants shouted on the tenth of December, 1848.[17] The masses knew they had a protector in the monarch; and dishonest merchants felt the bit in the bridle. But on the American continent—and the United States is not excluded —the supreme government has assumed economic and political obligations toward the gilded oligarchy, and the exploitation of employees, of workers and peasants is better guaranteed, is more complete, more cruel; it has no limits and is not punishable. On the American continent, the masses have no protector. A union, a syndicate, of governments (the Organization of American States—in which trafficking merchants and rulers are indistinguishable) has succeeded in setting up a new political and economic synthesis which Europe never has been able to do. [As the author previously indicated, the North Atlantic Alliance sought to achieve this. Now that it is breaking down, the Common Market, jointly operated by the governments and chiefly the great Franco-German coal and steel cartel, seems to be achieving this.—Translator] The politician, allied with the industrialist but subordinated to him, makes for well-oiled mechanized exploitation, multifaced and brutal.

* * *

Social dissenters and Kommunists obviously are wolves with the same hide. The Police Rulers so consider them and condemn them to death. Kommunism for them is an upsetting of the economic structures or protests against the usurers of today. The labor union is one of the most precious instruments to petition, to demand, and to recover what one has been robbed of by the stratagems of social and political Big Business. The labor union needs spokesmen and finds them without having to hunt for them. The labor union spokesman, like the people's spokesman, is always a strong man, perhaps the strongest

51

of all men, because his words are the words of thousands and sometimes of everybody. A spokesman is the steadfast expression of the collective will. But labor spokesmen are unarmed people—just the opposite of the Police Rulers, who well know the value of their weapons and the parapets from which they are fired. Out of that disparity spring psychological antagonisms, both social and political, between the two bands. To speak for others is to have authority, the one authority the Police do not have. But in the hour of conflict in the streets, it is the spokesman of labor, of the people, who dies. The Police win! The reasoning of the Government is made of lead, thunder, blood, and silence. ("The army under General Cavaignac intervened and imposed reason," commented with all naïvete a Chilean writer [referring to a European episode] in *El Mercurio*, Santiago de Chile, October 17, 1954.)

* * *

This news about social agitators executed in the middle of the street with the title "Kommunists," or merely branded with the useful appellation, leads us to the related question of popular leaders contemptuously called *"demagogues."*[18] Outside of the syndicalist leaders, this type sprouts from the social humus: its flower, its symbol, its banner. The masses also produce their spokesmen outside any union or brotherhood. (The concept of "people" differs much in sociology and politics. Politically speaking, the inhabitants of a country are divided among "the insiders," or those persons who govern and who obtain illicit profits from those who govern, and the masses, who do not enjoy these privileges and do not desire them. Politically speaking, the people are this independent mass, which can express an opinion, criticism, or praise. The insiders are no longer part of the people. They were a part of the people so long as they remained independent. The people, like a mother, hand over the government to them. Once in the government, they are disassociated in order that they may be judged. This is a process of provisional segregation, methodical separation, a parenthesis for those who are to be judged.)

People abused by the Police Rulers move in great waves, and their dynamism increases until they become a tidal wave. At any stage of their struggle the people produce spokesmen, those who have the clearest intelligence or most energetic determination, or can create the greatest emotional fervor. *A leader* is always a superior person, even though his superiority is not immediately visible beyond this pulling power. His psychological finesse permits him to feel the deep pulse of the people. His intellectual maturity permits him to transform these perceptions into a program of political action. His spiritual loftiness is invested with a certain suicidal quality which carries him forward to the dangerous post, to where are posted the machine-guns of the police. The people follow him, because he and the people complete each other. There is a sort of pact of sacrifice in which the people glorify their leader before destroying him. And they kill him because through the death of the leader, the people grow and the leader is immortalized.

Popular movements are bathed in blood and energized by blood. One can say that without this spilled blood, the people could not find their own true road. The blood is mingled with the dust. In this sense, the police fulfill a socio-biological or a medico-biological task: that of periodically inciting the masses to exercise their vitality and thus test their capacity to jump over the hurdles.

But at the same time a popular leader is a demagogue. Demagogy is the very marrow of leadership. Every act of a man of the people represents a critique of the status quo and an aspiration for the future. The leader who merely offers to tear down the fences is not a leader; he can be called a militia captain, a military strategist, but the political leader puts forward, in addition, a program of reconstruction. Upon the basis of this program, the leader makes promises, and to the extent he makes promises he is a demagogue. For those on the inside—for foreign exploiters—any promise is a lie, for they are never disposed to concede any reforms or change. From this point of view every leader is a charlatan. General Pedro Aramburu, provisional ruler of Argentina, wishing to ridicule the leaders, spoke March 20, 1957, "of the supreme social conquest of well-paid laziness" (*El Mercurio*, Santiago de Chile, March 27, 1957).

History demonstrates the opposite, for more than one leader has honored his program, and more than one leader has been a transformer of society. But the Police Ruler, with his preponderance of force, continues to confuse the leader with the irresponsible demagogue, and the demagogue with the Kommunist.

This Colonel Lazo knows. He buys more soap and polishes more wood for new crosses. For him the thief, the social agitator, the demagogues, the leaders of the people, old-time Kommunists, disturbers of the social peace—all are undesirable persons. There is still much "injustice" to be purged. He will do this new pruning even more happily when he remembers that the popular leader attacks

54

flanks that are especially tender for the Empire: he attacks the imperial flag. That other agitator—the union agitator —merely fought the voracity of the foreign enterprise, its privileges, and its pretensions of legal and racial superiority.

In contrast, the popular leader invested with other significance and wider obligations, goes further than attacks on commercial enterprise, small or big, and confronts the imperialist ambassador and the omnipresent flag in a struggle for national independence, with points of view that do not always bring the labor unions into action. It is this far trajectory of the popular leader's harpoon, his gaze on the soaring arrow flight, that provides the Police Ruler the means to combat him more effectively, for the latter finds in the foreign power his best ally. To the thick broth that the police have in their pot are added the onions and garlic thrown there by the Señor Ambassador. Both wait for the cooking, certain that the chicken, already stripped of feathers, will not escape, perhaps without effort will be deboned to improve the stew.

This leader, like the labor leader, dies in the street. A blind unnecessary solution: for the leader is not an individual important in himself. One dies, another arises. So long as there is a people, there will be a leader; and any leader whatever will always have superindividual strength, at times almost superhuman strength. The Police Ruler will never understand this; nor will the Señor Ambassador. And the leader will always be Kommunist: any and every leader, the one who dies and the one who springs forth from the blood of the one killed.

* * *

Doña Barbara, the heroine of Gallegos, took advantage

of midnight to move the boundary markers of her lands, every day augmenting the area of "her property." [Rómulo Gallegos is noted as a novelist and ex-Venezuelan President, deposed by Dictator Pérez Jiménez. His novel *Doña Barbara* is one of the great classics of Latin America.— Translator] In the same way the Police Ruler augments his brutishness in the middle of the night (or at midday, the result is the same), also his incomprehension of Kommunism and delinquency. We have observed that from the social agitator it is only a few small steps to the demagogue and to the leader: little shiftings of the verbal limits, a small idiomatic change, a smooth conceptual twisting. With this same shift, we are carried to other terrains which are being occupied and surveyed by the Gendarme, who is so motivated by affection for the social institutions and his obligations to the rulers above him. On more than one occasion, this roaming about and thieving (of military origin) will be done with good conscience, with a certain astute cleverness, in the belief that what he has in mind justifies and explains what he actually does. And so he comes into inevitable conflict with the leaders of the opposition. Whoever they are—oppositionists or conspirators— it is all the same. Bourgeoisie or not, aristocrats or not, landowners or not, financiers, industrialists, agriculturists, merchants, if they stand in the way of the police, they are Kommunists. Any explanation? Yes: the . . . social institutions, or the defense of democracy, or because the interests of the Empire are in danger.

The Police Ruler also arrogates to himself Academic Rights. The exercise of political power generates virtues that are nonpolitical. The high post implies talent, and the Police Ruler displays it. The high post implies culture, and the Police Ruler exudes it when he speaks; no, I beg pardon, not when he speaks, when he writes.

The highest literary quality is implicit in the functioning of government. Reader, have you not listened on the radio to those outpourings of "Fourth of July" orations by the police rulers? Or when an international conference is inaugurated? Speeches and magniloquent messages—full of meaty economic and social wisdom, which, though written by the best brain of the country, bear the signature of the Police Ruler? The critics, deeply moved, applaud fervently; the newspapers laud the discourse and the author (that is to say, the one who reads it). The intellectuals know that the Ruler has not written it; but the public reading of it makes it the property of the one who presents it, and since the Police Ruler reads it as his own, there is no way to evaluate his intellectual capacity or his ability as a writer or a stylist. (Waldo Frank comes to our assistance. Referring to the presidential campaign in the United States, he says: "The words have little meaning. They are generalizations and do not shine. The whole world knows that Eisenhower has not written his speech, that it is full of words he can scarcely pronounce, that he would never use in private conversation. But the entourage of 'speechwriters' have purposely made the phrases a bit heavy and have used great care that the speech will not be brilliant." [*Marcha*, Montevideo, October, 1956])

For there is the scholarly touch, i.e., the creative faculty, the talent to choose what is good and bad in the language, the right to define and blend words together, the right to invent new semantics—the word Kommunism, for example: its variations, its parallels, its purposes. And you will see the most unlikely persons named in the documents of the efficient typists and secretaries: they are the conspirators of yesterday, the Kommunists of today, the murdered of the day after tomorrow.

* * *

Thus far we have seen beaded on the Kommunist string persons engaged in what are universal activities: thieves, people who cause social ferment; social agitators, those who belong to labor unions; labor union officials, individuals who have the talent of leadership; the heads of the opposition to the Police Ruler, the conspirators. But the Police Rulers do not stop there. Following the threads of conspiracies, they have come upon a whole crop of new concepts. For conspiracy is rebellion, insubordination, nonconformity, accusation. Thereupon in our countries there appear a conglomeration of people never actually involved in conspiracy, who nevertheless fill the streets and deafen the ears with their yells and break windows and shout against the Police Ruler. It is Youth, the university students and those who never were and never can be students. They belong to the age in life which upholds in a lofty fashion the dignity of the human species. They uphold it with gallantry. Youth is still the man with the impetus to achieve, with a vocation for what is decent, and, for this reason, is stern and intransigent.

Youth, especially in the universities in Latin America, has taken as his own the demolishing of the Police Rulers. Youth is the first to ridicule them, the first to fight them, the first to curse them. Youth, also, is the first to contribute his own blood. Not because he is an idealist: the idealist is a spectator who prepares the future. Youth rather is spiritual in his make-up, and the man of spirit is a doer.

University youth in Latin America lives, in the here and now, the moral values necessary for his inner growth; he lives them now—yes, they still live—moral values which many adults have forgotten. Youth wants for himself and demands from everybody fidelity to purity, rectitude, manliness. Youth demands conduct more than he does ideas. He demands justice right now. And every day of the year, the truth. And for his country, unabridged sovereignty. Youth holds not so much to a Sociology based on economic fundamentals, but to an imperative Ethic. He does not value the material; he has no preference for material values. He is not moved by sensuality and does not fall into vices. He laughs at money and those who spend it. He has no talent for the feed-bag. He is romantic, because he still believes in Honor. And that means suicide. And there in the street when the student shouts his contempt and spits in the face of the political trickster, he faces the terrible Authority in full regalia: he who sells out the country and he who comes to buy it.

The Police Ruler hates Youth because he is his greatest enemy, perhaps his only enemy. Thus, as a result, Youth cannot fail—yes, he too—to be Kommunist. In fact, Youth has been so branded officially since 1918 when the Argentine students drew up in Córdoba a program of action that looked beyond the universities to the political developments in the country and the imperialist blows every day coming closer. Or at the least, Youth is accused of being manipulated by Kommunists. Or, even better, obeying Kommunist orders, dictated by radio from a foreign country. Pérez Jiménez was obliged to put down Kommunist riots with machine guns, killing fifteen-year-old students. Laureano Gómez and Rojas Pinilla left many adolescent bodies strewn in the streets—to save the social institutions. Castillo Armas rounded up a group of unarmed students in the center of Guatemala City and murdered a dozen Kommunists. [Pérez Jiménez, bloodthirsty and thieving dictator of Venezuela, was decorated by Eisenhower and held up by John Foster Dulles as a model that other Latin American executives should imitate. Laureano Gómez, of Colombia, ultraconservative and president, had been the most outspoken pro-Nazi and anti-United States element in Latin America, but immediately after World War II became the pet of General Marshall and the State Department, against whom the fury of the 1948 Bogotazo (or mass uprising) was especially directed. Rojas Pinilla, a subsequent Police Ruler of Colombia, slaughtered students and tens of thousands of peasants before being kicked out. Castillo Armas of Guatemala, with the aid of the Pentagon, the C.I.A., and the State Department overthrew elected President Jacobo Arbenz on the false charge that he was a Communist. Castillo was assassinated about a year later. He was one of the most contemptible of all the Police Rulers of the Americas.—Translator]

The university students of Cuba, in arms against the Army of Occupation, were also Kommunists. Obviously Latin America is lost; it is pack-jammed with Kommunists. Every day new Kommunist disturbances occur. People are now being born Kommunist! But the protection of God is not lacking: there, machine gun in hand, are the Police Rulers to save us.

* * *

There happens to be a form of Kommunism, quiet-voiced, harmoniously garbed, which is difficult to discern. This is the Kommunism disguised in every civic activity, better said in every civic demand. From the opposing viewpoint, every civic demand is considered antimilitarist. This is another peculiar aspect of Latin American life for, however much Europeans talk of militarism, the phenomenon over there does not have the same social and political characteristics as among us. Here the militarist is our daily diet. In America, no matter how much has already been said it will never be out of place to speak of militarism and antimilitarism.

At the beginning of this chapter we said it was not absolutely necessary that a Police Ruler be a professional militarist. In fact there is a certain antagonism between the gendarmerie and the essence of what is military. The militarist chooses a profession to which he devotes his whole life, physically and spiritually. His profession presupposes the social fact of war, and his task consists in apprenticeship for that end, exercise in the art of combat. The militarists cannot take a position on the sociological aspects of any problem; it does not correspond to their role, nor is it of any advantage for them to do so; they consider war as a social service, without repugnance or painful thought, in fact they can have no philosophy. (An illustrious exception was the Spanish Republican army man, General Vicente Rojo, who defended Madrid. *La Guerra en Sí* [War in Itself] is the name of a massive study about the sociology of war, the first part of his *Tríptico de la Guerra* [The Triptych of War] first published in Cochabamba, Bolivia, in 1953, where he lived during part of his glorious days in exile. In 1954 this three-volume work was reproduced with the title *Culminación y Crisis del Imperialismo* [The Culmination and Crisis of Imperialism] by Editorial Periplo, Buenos Aires.)

War is waged between enemy peoples, between nations which for the moment are enemies. The militarist is always concerned with this enemy, real or potential. "Sentinels of the Frontier," as Toynbee calls them, the militarists never plan to kill their fellow citizens. For this reason, the military man never discusses politics, even though he may have as much information at hand as the citizens of the country. Not that he is indifferent to ideologies; it is because his profession, by public accord, should respect them. Politics is a controversy about how to govern the country; and the militarists, as commanders of armed forces, cannot morally participate in the dispute.

At first sight it would seem that the military is not essentially contrary to civil life, but rather another aspect of it, or perhaps something quite apart, over and beyond civic life, neither denying it nor contradicting it. Is not the soldier in the case of war the defender and savior of civil life? Every citizen is or should be a potential soldier; just as every soldier, in spite of his uniform, should be a civilian in parenthesis.

One cannot say the same of the Police. The policeman does not devote himself to a profession; he practices a trade. For the gendarme there is no national or universal tradition; no frontier in dispute, no sovereignty in danger; there is no fatherland, no Empire, no profound history, no awareness of the Nation. Being a policeman is the activity of men to whom are assigned the duties of keeping order in the streets and, in certain cases, arresting delinquents. The elemental service they render is on the surface and requires no knowledge of mathematics; traffic rules, yes; pugilistic experiences, yes. But, they do bear arms and are authorized to use them and, in using them, must justify the use or abuse of them. Human lives are at the discretion of the police. The arms are given them to repel the attacks of the over-enthusiastic or delinquents. The task of the police is to repel and to arrest, but those he repels and arrests are his fellow citizens.

Basically here is the difference between the policeman and the militarist. The militarist not only prepares for the defense of the fellow citizen; at a given hour—the hour of combat—he is the most valiant and the most obedient of all citizens; while in contrast, the gendarme ignores all questions relating to the fatherland and looks upon the demonstration or shouting citizen as an enemy—even though the compatriot may be demonstrating or shouting in the name of the fatherland. The gendarme, civically a sexual neuter, has the function of dealing out blows; his charm is in beatings, in trampling the crowd with his horse, in throwing water from fire hoses; of opening the valves of tear gas, of showering chests with bullets, machine-gunning. To wound fellow citizens or kill fellow citizens is a foreseen accident and is often inevitable in the street agitations the gendarme faces. The policeman is thus an apprentice who years later may be the Ruler.

Hence, it is evident that between the military and the police there is only one thing that might lead to misinterpretation: the bearing of arms and the right and obligation to use them. But the militarist carries his as an adornment, and uses them in case of war. The policeman uses his revolver and his rifle as a happy daily sport. Thus, any civilian can become a policeman; all that is necessary is that he be armed and provided with the traffic rules and be taught how to speak of "social institutions." But also, unfortunately, any military man (Oh, Colonel Lazo!) can

63

lower himself to the police level when he forgets his profession and all that is elevated and moral in it. The result is confusion. That is why "militarism" is understood to be a sort of police mania with Rulers. But military government is not the same as police government, and the Police Ruler of whom we have been talking can be either a civilian or a militarist. The prototype of the Police Rulers in Guatemala used to be the lawyer who took over, saying he hated the Army. Thus Manuel Estrada Cabrera ruled the country thirty-two years and did not leave an opponent alive. He killed them as "Kommunists." The Yankees loved him. He was the one who made possible imperialist expansion by giving to the United Fruit Company, then just being born (1904), the only port built with state funds and the only railroad owned by the nation.

Guatemala has suffered from more Police Rulers than the one here mentioned. Perhaps that is why our literature on the subject is of such high quality. From Carlos Wyld Ospina's *El Autócrata* (The Autocrat), 1929, passing on to *Ecce Pericles*, by Rafael Arévalo Martínez (1945), to the world-renowned novel of Miguel Angel Asturias, *El Señor Presidente* (1945), Guatemalan thinkers have held a post of honor. In second rank can be placed my 1936 essay, *Las Cuatro Raíces del Servilismo* (The Four Roots of Servility), which considers the question in its psycho-sociological aspects.

This business of pinning the label of "militarism" on police street-tasks has its explanation. Some policemen actually have used the uniform to hide their trade. The exploits of the gendarmerie thus disguised are thereby blamed on the Army. And in some Latin American lands, the Army has come to be hated. The Police Ruler has

64

known how to capitalize on these emotional results. The trick of dressing up gendarmes as soldiers has not only succeeded in confusing civilian opinion, but the military as well. The latter came to believe that the wave of popular unrest was directed against their profession and, in critical moments, the militarists and police have joined in common defense in confused street situations, something from which the Señor Presidente has profited.

* * *

We recognize, therefore, one type of antimilitarism—a false antimilitarism—which arises from antagonism against the pseudo-militarism of the police. But in Latin America there is another political phenomenon, which we can also call "militarization," that consists of a certain governmental tendency to extend military regulations and methods into the civil sphere. Sometimes this is the result of manifestations of social unrest, hence is a transitory measure; but sometimes the purpose is to impose permanently on the civilians a martial posture—as when hospital services are militarized, or transport and post office services, or school establishments. For governments that proceed in this manner, the most obvious way to militarize is to put the whole country in uniform. This sort of militarization in turn generates another kind of antimilitarism, which we shall call "*civilista.*" *Civilismo*, in effect, opposes any injection of what is military into what is legitimately civilian.

A third form of militarism is the "military coup" (*militarada*), i.e., the sudden violent eruption of the militarists into the offices of the rulers, either civilian or military. This is the well-known phenomenon in Latin America —the *cuartelazo* or barracks revolt. The troops take over the power and replace the politicians. At times the generals are the actors; sometimes the sergeants are. The deed is the same. Faced by these militarists, the public, however, is not of one mind. They repudiate those kicked out and their friends; all who believe that the change will better their social, political, or economic positions applaud frenziedly. It is especially amusing to observe the antics of the lawyers faced with such legal bankruptcy. They justify the *cuartelazo* with an abundance of juridical excuses, while some colleagues vomit vituperation at the usurpation of the public power. It is not difficult, years later, to see the first (and the second ones) being forced to change their arguments when another military coup alters the situation. This form of militarism, the *cuartelazo*, has produced its own peculiar form of anti-militarism; the juridical.

In other instances, there is what I call *militaritis*, which is the aggravating intrusion of the militarists into the general life of the country. We speak of those epochs in which the military openly lean heavily on the budget, to the point of preventing the normal development of other spheres of national life. Various causes account for this. Some times it springs from real or fancied war dangers; at other times it is due to personal greed, when army chiefs see personal profit by purchasing arms. Irregularity can also come about through precarious political situations, in which the government needs to adulate the armed forces in order to affirm or prolong its legal period, and the militarists then "collect," in the form of juicy desserts, for their loyalty to the regime. This military inflation generates its special kind of adversary: institutional anti-militarism, exhibited by technicians who denounce it as a dangerous abnormality.

There remains finally a type of militarism called "Prussianism." This is the tendency to recognize the militarists as the only gentlemen in social life, the only creators of culture, the only statesmen. "We were born to command," said a military bigwig in a Spanish theatrical farce of the eighteenth century. Jorge Vigón, military theoretician of Spanish Falangism, repeats it complacently.[19] On this side of the Atlantic, the Venezuelan mountaineers shouted to Páez in 1830: "General, you are *La Patria!*"[20]

Taking these sayings literally, the army monopolizes for itself the command of the country and excludes civilians implacably. Prussia seems to have been, if not the initiator of this system, the country which gave it relative validity as a result of the national successes from such military control during the last century—up until Verdun, the first stage of the great disaster. Already in the eighteenth century Mirabeau came to say that Prussia is "not a country with an army, but an army with a country."[21] The antimilitarism adverse to this trend is largely philosophical, holding that obedience of the soldier does not represent the essence of man.

The forms of antimilitarism mentioned here are antidotes for military abnormalities. But in the history of ideas is recorded still another kind of antimilitarism which not only opposes pathological manifestations of militarism, but rejects the military entirely, denying the need for the institution of war-making and proclaiming that it is possible to suppress the social phenomenon of war. The European *anarchists* of the nineteenth century

67

and a type of revolutionary syndicalism of the beginning of this century preached an antimilitarism that is actually *anti-war-ism*.

So what? Our Police Ruler and his deputy Colonel Lazo call all kinds of civic protest and all these types of antimilitarism Kommunist. This is another false label, a strategem to confuse or win sympathy; for no Communist, from Plato to Stalin, ever urged the suppression of the army or disdain for the military.

* * *

But the most audacious political-philological tactic of the Police Ruler is to call Kommunist every person—especially every politician—who expresses sympathy for the poor, the disinherited, for those who do not belong to any social establishment, for the proletariat whatever its origin, for workers in general. When we reach this point, all possibility of any ideological explanation of policy vanishes, and we are left with only the sight of the policeman in shirtsleeves. Since the Gendarme is primarily a guardian of the property of others—a well-paid, well-fed guardian—one of his aims is to maintain his superior status as such a guardian in the eyes of those who seem to be the potentates inside and outside the country. We accept the word *oligarchy* to designate the powerful, though actually we are dealing with government by a small handful. Thanks to the Police Ruler these few are able to maintain their domination and exploitation of the great majority of the inhabitants.

No one is better able to distinguish between gentlemen and servants than the Police Ruler. His function consists in exalting the former and keeping the others in the traditional role of sheep. A rooted contempt for everything plebeian, for the people, characterizes the Police Rulers and those preparing to become such. It makes no difference that the gendarme comes out of the ranks of these same plebes. The past is past. He is interested in the future, in his sons and daughters. They must be married off well. They must enter the upper social circles, rub elbows with "worthwhile people." Many White Russians, many marquesses and barons—people without offspring and come down in the world—wander about these Americas, who, if well paid, can produce grandchildren with different colored skins. There is many an elegant gentleman in the stock exchange, around the gambling tables, or too deeply in debt to the hotel to be thrown out—beautiful examples of decadent races. Races which can be toned up by Indian or *mestiza*, Negro or Zamba blood. The Police Ruler wishes to get into the glittering salons of gold and silk, where he can sacrifice his daughters to the golden calf or the pedigreed bull. Fat chance that the Police Ruler will sympathize with the plebes, with the poor!

The early preaching of republicanism in Latin America was a sentimental fiction. The monarchical tradition predominated in the conscience of many; and there has been no lack of "liberators," many of them plebeian, who wished to restore kings or emperors on this savage soil, crossed by great torrential rivers. But monarchical proposals never triumphed; even so, if the republican fiction finally won out, the rulers and the powerful continued to ape the customs of the European courtiers. All these Latin American oligarchies suffer from aristocratic nostalgia, seeking illustrious names for the telephone books, trying to rub out of the family records the names of forefathers who had unfortunate brushes with the law. Is this not true, Doctor Calcagno? (I am reminded of the magisterial lectures of Doctor Alfredo D. Calcagno in La Plata Normal School, in which he explained to upper-class students this mania for glorious ancestors, which paralleled the mania to forget or deny all kinship with those who had practiced any form of delinquency.)

And the upstart flamboyant politicians who dutifully serve this oligarchy—among them the Police Ruler—vie for the chance to punish the plebes, to keep them at a distance, to uphold the laws against revolutionary blows, and prolong their privileges and advantages to the point of tugging at the hair of God himself in behalf of the rich. This is how medals are won. And this is why the most timid effort to ease the situation of the poor causes such a ridiculous reaction in the topmost bureaus. A certain air of Versailles, in the form of costumes and decorations, disguises these distinguished mandarins. They dream of fulfilling Spengler's prognostication: the hangmen of today will be the dukes of tomorrow. They know very well that *inside they are lackeys,* and in their own souls they smile at their own difficulty in hiding their livery with decorations. Livery of presidents!

NOTES TO CHAPTER II

1. Laureano Vallenilla Lanz, "El gendarme necesario," in *Cesarismo Democrático* (Caracas, 1929), p. 175.

2. Robert E. Guyer, *Imperialism.*

3. *El Mercurio* (Santiago de Chile), September 9, 1957. Reuters Cable from London.

4. *Acción* (Montevideo), August 27, 1958. UPI Dispatch.

5. Juan José Arévalo, *Escritos Politicos y Discursos* (Political Writings and Speeches) (Definitive edition, Havana, 1953), pp. 65-68.

6. "Ladron [Thief]. The true meaning of the Latin term *latro, onis,* from which the Castilian word is derived, was a mercenary soldier in the imperial guard. Among the *latrones* of Rome, just as among the mercenaries of Spain in the Golden Age, because of lack of pay, demoralization was introduced, and they became highwaymen, which explains the transformation of the meaning of the word." Roberto Vilchis Acuña, *Semántica Española* (Spanish Semantics) (Buenos Aires, 1954), p. 25.

7. Bernhard Groethuysen, *La formación de la consiencia burguesa en Francia durante el siglo XVIII* (Formation of the Bourgeois Conscience in France during the Eighteenth Century) (México, 1943) , p. 558.

8. Robert A. Brady, *La riqueza tras el poder* (The Wealth behind the Power) (México, 1945), p. 330.

9. *Clarín* (Santiago), March 29, 1957.

10. Gregorio Bustamante, *Una satrapía en el Caribe* (A Caribbean Satrap) (México, 1949). See also my "Prólogo en Disidencia" (Prologue in Dissidence) , in Horacio Ornes, *Desembarco en Luperón* (México, 1956).

11. Harvey O'Connor, *El imperio del petróleo* (The Empire of Oil) (México, 1956), p. 362.

12. Vicente Sáenz, *El fraude del anticomunismo* (The Fraud of Anti-Communism) (México, 1953) . Especially page 119f. of *Auscultación Hispanoamericana* (México, 1954) . Cf. O'Connor, p. 414.

13. *El Mercurio*, April 27, 1957.

14. Rodney Arismendi, the translator of this quotation [into Spanish] confesses that he took it from Palme Dutt, *Fascisme et revolution. Para un prontuario del dólar (Fascism and Revolution, an Examination of the Dollar)* (Montevideo, 1947), p. 21. George Seldes also translates this passage with slight variations in *Mil Norteamericanos, los dictadores de los Estados Unidos* (Buenos Aires, n.d.), pp. 148-49; and in *Mil Norteamericanos,*

71

los verdaderos gobernantes de los Estados Unidos (Buenos Aires, 1958).

15. "Jesus was also one of the many who have revolted in the name of Justice and Law."—Giovanni Lerda, *Influencia del Cristianismo en la economía* (Buenos Aires, 1936), p. 52.

16. Lerda, p. 78.

17. Georges Gurvitch, *El concepto de clases sociales, de Marx a nuestros días* (The Concept of Social Classes, from Marx to Our Day) (Buenos Aires, 1957) , p. 45.

18. Attacks on the opposition leaders under the pretext of combating "banditry."—Brady, p. 354.

19. Jorge Vigon, *Teoría del militarismo* (Theory of Militarism) (Madrid, 1955) , p. 64.

20. Vallenilla Lanz, p. 212.

21. Edward Grigg, *La politica exterior británica* (British Foreign Policy) (Madrid, 1945), p. 52.

III.

THE UNITED STATES AND ITS ANTI-KOMMUNISM

Experience has proved that foreign influence is one of the most pernicious enemies of republican government.

—George Washington

We are doing everything possible to convince our children that the most important thing in life is to get fat.

—Valentín Letelier

As in a serialized novel, we put aside the story of the Police Rulers and abruptly step into a different world, very different in its beliefs, its style, its methods, but so close to the other that it is immersed in it; we can say the people there live, stand together over the same victim, without danger of quarreling, like two parasitic plants that compete in silence for the sap of the leafy tree. It is the world of businessmen, of big business, of entrepreneurs, captains of industry, multimillionaires and their representatives and superintendents, stewards and majordomos; the world of capitalists and their beagle hounds—all persons who now speak English, who entered through the wide doors of the United States, abandoning Nordic Europe, its customs and its speech, and who adopted the standard of liberty, of absolute liberty, liberty undisturbed by prejudices. This liberty knows how to seize what is before it, that which is most brilliant or carries the most weight so that one has more strength than his neighbor, bigger claws, sharper teeth—and can buy immunity from the sheriff.

Here we come to admire a new psychological landscape, less rustic than that we discovered in the dense tropical world of the Gendarmes. The contours, the aerodynamics, the better distribution of the masses (in cellars), the human shadows controlled with a perfect sense of gradation to the infinite. Safer depths (again the cellars) and a play with a perspective of not less than ninety-nine years. A different psychological landscape where the human types are in marked contrast with the village gendarmes in our world, the colonial palace customs, with their Indian plumage or their ostentatious Spanish-style uniforms, the political bosses and generals with fat cheeks and teeth, round irritable faces, chests bejeweled with decorations.

In this new world, à la Velásquez, the clothes are different: silk predominates, jewels are more delicate and discreet, faces are slim and smiling, tables are aglow with lordly cut-glass; the walls panoplied with foreign coats of arms and portraits of ad hoc forefathers. Nevertheless, in spite of the contrasts, these dwellers are moved by the same obsession as the Gendarmes: the juridical and philological obsession about a certain thing called Kommunism.

74

Perhaps it is not the Gendarme's madness for peniten- tiaries and catacombs, where everything is solved by in- quisitional tortures and pious crosses, but nevertheless it is a punitive obsession that resorts to legal persecutions and courts-martial, supported by will-executing lawyers and newspaper men chorusing in C major, who attest to everything, if paid off.

In another way the Police Rulers and the Millionaire Tartuffes are alike: in the primitiveness of their culture. Each finished the primary grades in their native country and climbed up in a world where notions of geography and history were unnecessary. They jumped into a system in which another kind of physics and mathematics was of value: a sportive physics and adding-machine mathematics of mechanized rapidity and infinite accumulation, blind to all limits, an acoustics of deaf men oblivious to human clamor featured by magnetic audacity and good hoofs. Lithe and sure, the feline falls upon the prey. There are the physics and mathematics of success, an empty success, for it is a success of winning out over your neighbor, tak- ing advantage of him, getting the better of him, as in a circus filled with a large troupe of performers and the stink of galloping show-horses.

But besides a physics and a mathematics, like the gen- darmes they also have the philological characteristics of being obsessed with words. We watch them gathered about a gambling table talking, talking and trading chips. The millionaires, they too, know what Kommunism means. At times they leave the salon and go, like Colonel Lazo, to the edge of the river of culture; they climb on the same rock and amuse themselves watching the brown flood waters or the lovely spray, and they point out the things

75

floating by, absorbed and fearful, like children, fascinated by the force of the torrent and the uneven roar. From that vantage point, they pronounce words about objects passing by, trying out their experiments in vocabulary and shouting out the hidden significance at the top of their lungs.

They, like Colonel Lazo, discovered the social, cultural, and anthropological subject called Kommunism! But it is a different Kommunism! A Kommunism with novel characteristics, richer in metaphors, and with more sibilant phonetics. This may be because the multimillionaires and their commercial agents look at the world through lenses of different thickness and color, because they listen in the midst of the hoarse respiration of anxiety. Thus they come up with unexpected attitudes, at times disconcerting, which will please the police, and which take them arm in arm dancing, dancing to the end of the ball, from pirouette to pirouette, with a single music and a single song.

* * *

Just as Colonel Lazo led us by the hand to the essence of what is a gendarme, we now need a participant who will serve to guide us among the heel-tapping and gentility of this millionaire setting. We should like to find one of flesh and blood so as to leave story-telling to one side. By invoking the Statue of Liberty, our search may be brief. We have him! Here he is! We don't even have to change his name. The person we seek is named *Spruille Braden.*

He is known from Mexico to Argentina, from Guatemala to Cuba, even in Chile and Bolivia. The name Braden is a name synonymous with tin and copper: their South American metallic vibrations are not lost wherever we stand, at whatever altitude. They come from that pioneer named William Braden, who arrived with the heavy flight of a buzzard in the mighty Chilean mountains, swooped down leaving a little pile of dollars, to exploit the ores of "El Teniente." That was back in 1904.

Brought up in various climes, educated bi-lingually, bookkeeper during the day and dancer of tangos at night, this Don Spruille grew up and became fat, traveling from south to north and returning north to south, until he came to merit the office of the Great Official in the diplomatic service of the United States. I knew him in March, 1946, when he was serving the interests of Wall Street in that producer of dollars known as Cuba. He came then to Guatemala, heading the Yankee mission when I took my presidential oath of office. Months later he financed and directed a political campaign against the Shirtless of Argentina who were shouting their nascent Peronismo.[1]

Promoted to the post of Under Secretary of State for Latin American affairs, he was denounced as a Kommunist sympathizer and was thrown out. My Washington Ambassador came to me to beg for a decoration that would soften the fall of this personage, and there went the Order of the Quetzal, because the truth is Mister Braden was a good friend of Guatemala during the first hours of our Revolution. "Guatemala is one of our greatest hopes on the American continent. It is the country that understands democracy just as we conceive of it," Braden told a Guatemalan diplomat in Washington in June, 1946.

But after Braden got his 1947 decoration, and until the events of 1953 and 1954, the winds changed. From an alliance against Hitler alive, the United States had gone on to an alliance with Hitler dead. The anti-Kommunist breeze had become a hurricane, blown up by the big mouth of McCarthy, and the rain of word-projectiles began falling upon the earth: Kommunism, pro-Kommunism, pre-Kommunism, proto-Kommunism, philo-Kommunism, quasi-Kommunism, crypto-Kommunism, semi-Kommunism, moving-toward-Kommunism, larval-Kommunism, spectral-Kommunism. . . . The verbal torrent fell on public officials and ex-officials. A sensation of evil and fear transformed the consciousness of many Yankees. Mister Braden was not asleep; he was searching for an umbrella, a sponge, a towel, a rubber eraser. Finally he believed he could save himself by also raising the alarm —he too—against the Kommunists, their parents, allies, namesakes, their homonyms and paronyms. No better victim could be found than this same Guatemala, the same Guatemala which had decorated him. It was in October, 1953, that Doctor Jagan, Creole leader of British Guiana, won the election. Mister Braden denounced both Jagan and Arbenz as preparing to bombard the Panama Canal and utilized the occasion to denounce the Kommunism recently installed in Bolivia.

Mr. Braden's attempt to wash off the old spots did not help him. In December, 1953, a McCarthy commission put him on the bench of the accused.

"No; the Kommunist was not I, the Kommunists were others," Mister Braden would have liked to cry out from his troubled soul. But he could not talk that way because he was before the tribunal of the State Inquisition. Badly advised by the "psychology" of tin and copper, which ennobles others, he had the bad taste to denounce his own colleagues in the Department of State. He said they were "uniformly antagonistic toward him with regard to private property." And he added, "To say the least, all had socializing tendencies."[2]

We are now treading new ground. The Police Rulers call thieves and social agitators Kommunists; that is their field. Plutocrats like Mister Braden call *Socialists* Kommunists. All are the same, or at least it is convenient that the diverse be considered identical. The aim is to create confusion, fabricate mix-ups, entangle concepts, rub out boundaries, pile up diverse words as is done in the jails when prisoners of different categories are mistaken for each other. At the present hour a new political strategy—a new technique of semantics—piles up and stirs words together and puts them to boil in the pot. Stick your fork into the stew and whatever you get, it will always be a Kommunist.

This is what Mister Braden did to sidle out of a jam; it was hardly a hiccough or a sneeze he delivered. What he said about his fellow workers—almost all of them high chiefs—pointing to them as accomplices of Kommunism by calling them Socialists, was already a mental norm of the agile tango dancer. We can prove this by a much more recent document. It was October 12, 1957, in Washington when he received the prize of the Fundación de las Américas awarded by the Inter-American Press Association.[3] In his speech, Braden spoke of human dignity and liberty and, with a certain presumption, of *"our twenty-one Republics. . . ."* In men who have a religious opinion toward private property, the word "our" is frightening. But we are getting out of line. The dignity and liberty which Mr. Braden explained on this occasion were a prod-

79

uct of material goods: production, consumption, transportation, and money. Dignity and liberty were the juice and aroma of concrete goods. Those modern states with "socializing tendencies" were attacking that dignity and liberty. Those who sought to arrogate to themselves the control of the stream of purchases and the ocean of sales by putting taxes on those goods, according to his speech, were attacking life itself. Socializing tendencies were not only a threat against millions, but the danger of death for the millionaire. Socialism is the tomb of liberty! And naturally he did not fail to cite Jefferson, just as others similarly bring us the words of Jesus of Galilee himself.

Mister Braden became dramatic that October 12. It was all right that Columbus had been born in Genoa, the city of usurers, and that the men of New York feel themselves to be compatriots of the Genoese or of the Venetians who, in usury, don't bring us the tail end, if we are to believe Francisco de Quevedo. [Quevedo was a Spanish satirist, born in Madrid in 1580.—Translator] But for the North Americans to take over October 12 as a patriotic holiday and confuse the *Mayflower* with the *Santa Maria* and make use of Columbus for kitchen tasks and use his sword (as that of Bolívar) as the mast for "Continental" flags and use the memory of them as a theme for anti-Kommunism . . . goes far beyond what is customarily called "poetic license."

Obviously Mr. Braden abused that license with considerable usury. He spoke of life and death. He and all his people preferred to be hungry rather than lose their dignity. It takes much imagination, a great deal of imagination, to picture a stubby pig-like millionaire dying of hunger. The millionaires produce hunger in ton lots. The erudite Brazilian Josué de Castro once said, "Hunger is a plague created by man."[4] The North American Thomas Stokes denounced the policies of the Republican Party of the United States, as being the first to create hunger and soon to strangle the hungry. Betty Kirk, reminding her compatriots of this denunciation, dilates on it by saying that this is the policy in Latin America of the Department of State under the Republican Party, that in addition it dedicates itself to overthrowing governments with the false slogan of anti-Communism.[5] So multimillionaires fabricate hunger, but do not suffer from it, nor do they even know it. They have never seen it passing by. This universal and plebeian miasma of hunger does not ride up the elevators of the Waldorf Astoria. Perhaps they invoke it because they do not know it. "We prefer hunger to loss of liberty"—the liberty to keep on accumulating millions, the liberty of misery, that is to say, of creating misery. But hunger is not enough expiation for Mr. Braden. His oratorical emotion, an uncontained whirlpool, caused him to say, "Any form of suffering, even *death itself*, is preferable to losing liberty!" Anybody who hears that millionaires are at the portals of hunger or are at death's door from hunger will put chicken on to stew.

In the last war, not to go far afield, millions of men died, but among the dead scarcely one body of a millionaire was found. Naturally they were not in the trenches. Nor were they under bombardment, for—who knows by what miracle?—the millionaires know beforehand where the bombs are going to fall. The millionaires who helped Hitler prepare the hecatomb did not die at Hitler's side. The millionaires of New York, heavily allied with German industrialists, did not die either. Nor those of London, nor those of Paris, nor those of Tokyo. That is why, when war is over, they are shaken by chills and fever, moved by the memory and statistics of the deaths, and cry out in the hour of peace for more deaths. Deaths by which they can halt the diffusion of reports on misery and hunger. And they are such enemies of "socializing tendencies" that they even confess themselves to be anarchists. "The individual," said Mr. Braden that dramatic October 12, "should be master of his destiny and the sole judge of his ambitions." Did you hear it? The individual. Watch out for the State! Be it an autocratic State or a socialistic state. *"The State always tends toward tyranny,"* added Mr. Braden. Except the Yankee State, of course, which century after century will continue being an inspiring democracy. Having heard these recriminations against the State, very much like those of Lenin or what presently we hear from the mouth of the Catholic Church, and listening to this or that invocation to death by hunger, around the Carthaginian banquet table, from moment to moment we wait to hear the pistol shot and see the lifeless body of the suicide rolling under the table. But no, men like Braden do not resort to suicide nor do they wish to die. He is using rhetorical fictions, making studied postures for the stage, *social fictions.* He speaks in this fashion in order that the major newspapers in "our twenty-one Republics" and those newspapers of those creators of liberty who are millionaires repeat his homily and clap their hands and burn incense before the altars of human liberty.

* * *

Persevering along these lines by which we have managed to discover such an unusual theory of hunger and death, let us have a look at *Standard Oil*, the vertebral column of the Empire, so as to explain a bit more about "socialistic tendencies." In 1944 the president of Standard Oil of Ohio was Mr. A. A. Stambaugh. The workers in the enterprise asked for a collective contract, a legitimate instrument of the struggle against hunger. Naturally another type of hunger. This is the hunger of homes where there are no banquets nor speeches nor theater pieces, nor photographers. A hunger that kills by lack of nutrition, but without noise. Mr. Stambaugh complained about these hungry ones, just as Goliath complained about David. "They were trying to introduce a collective contract as a club with which to beat the rich." Understand? "This kind of a contract . . . smells of Socialism and leads to Communism."[6] Understand? Mr. Stambaugh and Mr. Braden, one the president of an enterprise that is endeavoring to put by modest savings and the other the representative of those savings which lie in the vaults of New York, coincide in their prophecies. The Socialists and socializing tendencies lead to Kommunism.

It fell upon General Eisenhower, who discharged the difficult position of President of an Empire, to lower the words to base bellicose levels. In June, 1954, in one of his many speeches preparing for what was to happen to Guatemala, he used the phrase "despicable Socialism." The wrath of Eisenhower against Socialism is borrowed wrath, fictitious wrath. It is not the wrath of an army man, for if we are to believe Spengler, money and the army are antagonistic forces, and the cream of militarism—Prussianism —was Socialistic, disinterested and austere, as contrasted with British merchants, of Norman origin, devoted to money, experts in looting.

We are not hearing in Eisenhower, therefore, the voice of soldiers who speak with pride and honor, who despise self-enrichment and greed, who consider their lack of money still another trophy. No, in Eisenhower's voice we detect accents alien to the military man. It is the voice of New York millionaires, with little or none of the army accent, at a moment when they have need of the Gendarmes in showy uniforms to fool the children and distract the multitude. Eisenhower's wrath is civilian wrath; wrath of the clan, the race, the ethnos. It is archaic wrath: from the tombs. It is the wrath of those who never learned to relax. The Phoenician wrath that prefers to die . . . of thirst before it will *give a drop of water to the neighbor.* Eisenhower's voice is that of the master-singers of New York: those allied voices (a collective contrast neither more nor less) of the Cabot Lodges, and the Moors Cabots, and the Mackenzie Moors, and the Morgan MacKenzies, the Ford Morgans, and the Rockefeller Fords. The "despicable Socialism" of Eisenhower makes us recall the *"cursed democracy"* of Mr. David Parry back in 1903, when this gentleman served with the title of leader or president or representative of the North American Manufacturers Association.[7]

An aristocrat of Versailles, of those who in the middle of the seventeenth century laughed at the inexpert physicians and the Tartuffe priests, would have preferred to murmur against the "despicable traders" and the "cursed upstarts." Scarcely three centuries later, the merchants and the upstarts have taken the disguise of aristocrats and, entrenched in their false habiliments, wish to alter the phrase and put it in the mouths of new performers. Now the ostentatious militarists act on the stage, playing the

84

role of comedians, speaking the lines the millionaires want them to repeat. Despicable Socialism! Cursed Democracy!

*   *   *

Not merely hunger: wages and strikes are social problems of changing values. Within the United States they signify one thing; in Latin America quite another.

In 1914 Henry Ford set five dollars a day as a minimum wage for his workers. In 1955 these same Yankee workers have their own automobiles, refrigerators, television sets, book shelves. Magical Metropolitan industry! In contrast we continue under feudal slave agriculture, which grinds up men into waste pulp. When I began my presidential term in 1945 and visited the coffee zone of La Alta Vera Paz, I personally noted that the *mozos* (the farm hands or peons) earned four cents a day. [La Alta Vera Paz is a northern jungle province of Guatemala, with rich coffee and sugar plantations. To the north is Petén, still wild and untamed, but with many plantations, where one of the chief activities is the gathering of chicle for chewing-gum. Four cents was lower than the prevailing wage of that time, fifteen centavos a day.—Translator]

I spoke with one of the *mozos*. He was married and had five children. The children had no school or medicine. The popular Guatemalan Revolution—nationalist!—did not rest until it could offer these workmen a minimum wage that met their family needs. And schools. And hospitals. That is how our Kommunism began. They never called Henry Ford a Kommunist, for the North American workers belonged to another race and another political area of the world. They were metropolitan workers. The

85

workers of the south, on the other hand, are considered second-class human material; and their low wages are providing the prosperity of others there in the United States, and for some others here in Latin America.

They tell me that in the Dominican Republic—private property of an anti-Kommunist General [Trujillo]—once there was a desperate attempt to obtain better wages and the suicidal determination to say so in public. The following day the bodies of the "social agitators" appeared hanging from the trees. Each one had a sign tied to his feet: "My salary was raised." For all such problems, the Gendarme enjoyed the assistance of a Yankee lawyer, none other than the oldest son of Franklin D. Roosevelt, who was paid $60,000 a year. [This same Roosevelt who was employed by the bloody dictator Trujillo was named Under Secretary of Commerce by John F. Kennedy in 1963.—Translator]

On one occasion Trujillo gave the wife of Secretary of State Hull a necklace of real pearls, which he himself—Trujillo—lovingly placed on the neck of the great lady. This from the country which did not have a single penny more for its fellow citizens.

Trujillo was not unique in this hemisphere. Brazilian Ambassador Senor Assis de Chateaubriand gave Queen Elizabeth II a turquoise bracelet and a clip, in the name of Brazilian President Kubitschek. The presentation of the jewels was made during an audience granted to the diplomat at Buckingham Palace, according to an A.P. dispatch in *El Pais* (Montevideo) on August 6, 1958. [The wage scale of Brazilian peasants is perhaps even lower than in the Dominican Republic.—Translator]

More feared than any verbal request for increased

86

wages are *strikes* or the threat of strikes. The financial sensitivity of anti-Kommunism has written on this theme in capital letters. Kommunist are the laws that sanction strikes, the Congresses which propose or vote them, the rulers who promulgate them and enforce them, the newspaper men who support and applaud them. We are referring to Latin America, naturally. Because there the struggles between the governments and the workers are dressed in tragic clothes. Real battles are unleashed by certain armies against their fellow-citizen workers—battles not inscribed in the military history of the country, nor in the history of trade, but which have cost innumerable lives and created new cemeteries. They are battles of life and death, between the foreign enterprise, based on certain calculations in New York, and the workers who rent out their labor and their health. The Creole army is unshakably loyal to the company. The mission of Latin American armies—a tail of the Yankee Army now in the postwar era —has been concentrated on the task of protecting foreign commercial profits.

Right now, as I begin this book in October, 1957, the Peruvian army has been mobilized to put an end to a strike of workers at the Toquepala mine in the south of the country. This copper-mining enterprise belongs to the North American imperial American Smelting Corporation. Sixteen hundred Peruvian workers are asking for a wage increase. The president has declared the strike illegal and has mobilized the entire army. Land, sea, and air forces have gone into action. The marines have disembarked in the neighboring port of Ilo, with three destroyers at their back. War planes fly over the zone; for several hours fifty jet planes have zoomed overhead, tracing zigzags and curves. The death toll for the "enemy," that is, for Peruvian workers, has been six dead and twenty wounded, according to *La Gaceta* (Santiago de Chile), October 29, 1957, and *El Mercurio*, November 7, 1957.

The survivors went back to work. The imperialist enterprise continued paying the same low wages. The national army had performed its duty. The Police Ruler also. [This typical atrocity and servile conduct were displayed by President Manuel Prado backed by the APRISTA party, supposedly a people's party, which had the full support of the U.S. Embassy and the C.I.A. in recent national elections. Both the APRA leader, Haya de la Torre, and Prado had the unqualified help of the Department of State, the U.S. secret police agencies, and the Pentagon. But Prado was thrown out by a military coup a week before completing his term, to prevent Haya from taking office after a fraudulent election. The State Department got over its pique when the new gang of vandals promised to be even more anti-Kommunist than Prado and Haya de la Torre.—Translator]

Within the metropolitan territory, that is to say inside the United States, things happen in a different manner.[8] The social and economic dispute between capitalism and workers has characteristics and aspects different from those in colonial or, as they now call them, underdeveloped territories. At the beginning of United States capitalism, when the multimillionaires could not yet count on the White House, the struggle between owners and workers was terrible. Every large U.S. factory had private troops. They were hired gangsters, provided with arms outside law and the government, with machine-guns, pistols, and clubs.[9] They lived near the factory and awaited merely the signal to sally forth to "convince" the strikers. When Rockefeller and Theodore Roosevelt made peace, the factories no longer needed private troops; the troops of the State took care of the millions, that is to say, of order.

But as time went by, a sort of understanding came about between Yankee owners and Yankee workers. They began to sell stock to workers in each factory. "Despicable Socialism" was spreading its ideas so there was begun what is now called *the people's capitalism*. Thus the workers of the United States came to "participate" in the profits, and so put their O.K. on all that the enterprises did outside the country. The search and seizure of foreign raw materials is of interest to the people as well as to the multimillionaires. The investment of "profits and savings" in underdeveloped countries benefited some forty million Yankees, albeit in a small way. The Yankee multimillionaires have thus been able to count on "public opinion." (So peculiar is Yankee capitalism—and so world-wide— that it has swallowed the *charity handouts* of 456 million [Catholics of the entire world]—handed over by the Vatican for "investment." Clearly the unhappy Catholics, though involuntary "stockholders," do not participate in the celebration of dividends, which come back to the Vatican, and from the Vatican travel forth once more to New York. . . . And so on to the end of time.) Now the workers and capitalists don't quarrel; they converse—the dialogue is in English. They are engaged in the ancient, thousand-year-old tradition of splitting up the booty, a habit derived from the Viking raiders, who thus calmed their nerves and pacified their consciences.

But the Rockefeller-Theodore Roosevelt pact was not valid for Latin America. The workers (who speak Span-

89

ish, French, or Portuguese) are treated in a different way. A Yankee General has confessed that a short time ago his forces had lists of "Wet Backs" who had crossed the border clandestinely to be returned to Mexico by the harshest illegal methods. On the Panama Canal Zone there is one scale of wages for the Yankee worker and another for the Panamanian worker. The United Fruit Company does not have to modify this imperialist treatment in the three Republics where it operates. Not to know English is a defect, and this provides an excuse to reduce wages and salaries, thereby justifying new economic "classes" that conceal the racial and political discrimination. Many years will pass before the inferior race will be admitted as "stock owners" or participants. It will take three centuries until the Empire will have completed its present Nazi-Carthaginian phase. Until this period has gone by, the struggle for better wages, the disrespectful and "subversive" strike, will be characterized as Kommunist.

Naturally this goes also for any distribution of land. The Fifth General Assembly of the United Nations (1950) in theory can advise agrarian reform. A Secretary of State, Dean Acheson, can approve of it—when taken by surprise at the avalanche of new ideas and frightened by the clamor of two billion hungry people. A Supreme Court Judge, William Douglas, softened up by the truth, can suggest that the United States itself promote "social justice" not Communist, in underdeveloped peasant countries, according to *Diario de Centro América* (Guatemala), April 8, 1952.

But when Guatemala took the U.N. recommendation seriously and passed a land reform law, as in 1952, the words became deeds and virtue became a crime. When in

1953 Bolivia, tragic Bolivia, passed an agrarian law, it was bombarded with the most shameful words. The continental forces and the Inspectors of the Empire took it upon themselves to see that the matter did not go beyond a mere law. The Latin American landowners, with their feudal mentality, refuse to alter the basic nature of the economy. Agriculture, as an activity of people, makes no sense. The important thing is raw materials for the functioning of the Empire. The landholders here and the industrialist there are mutually necessary. And they assist each other without regard for frontiers. There are never lacking, neither here nor there, the close ties nor the voices of alarm. Thus it was that in 1952 when the Argentine Casa de la Cultura (House of Culture) for the tenth time denounced the "landholding oligarchy" and "imperialist domination" and asked for the liquidation of land monopoly and cried out for agrarian reform, the combat troops of the continent rushed to do battle, crying Kommunists.[10]

What in juridical philosophy is sovereignty in the politics of the trenches is nationalism, and in the markets is nationalization. The disgraceful postwar days have torn away the notions that clothed us and gave us our basic concepts. Now, as in autumn, the leaves are falling one by one. The industrialists who manufacture and package political and commercial recipes have put into storage as forbidden all that was once consumed under the honorable name of nationalism. The wakeful Latin American who still talks about this is exposed to punishment by an invisible electric death ray. Nationalism is the same as saying: customs barriers, independent industry, protection of the native citizen, exaltation of Creole life; and, also,

91

just prices for raw materials produced inside the country, insistence on commercial equality, defense of our money, reciprocity, respect, dignity. But all this slows up the flow of merchandise that comes from north to south; it disturbs the dialogue being carried on in English, the discussion of diplomatic privileges, the diminution of shameful Embassy privileges. And when we proceed from the concept to the act of nationalization, then the word piracy no longer serves, the big press speaks of exterminating massacres, without remembering the avalanches of Indians that descended upon the Spaniards when the latter went to sleep.

For this reason our future policy must be carried on with extreme caution; it is a case of never using disrespectful or suspected conspiratorial words, those suspected of serving to carry out extracontinental orders. On board a noun or on the rump of an adverb, Russia can stick her nose in. In addition, if we close our ports to the Yankee products and hold them in the customs and impose a few cents tax, and thus humiliate ourselves by imitating what the Frenchman or an Italian does . . . then there are unbearable reprisals that go far beyond words. To avoid this, we open the custom doors to the Yankees; floors waxed, carpets spread out, the porters scraping and bowing, eyes lowered, their thoughts unuttered. *The Spanish notice* which told people to knock before entering, has been torn down. Our house is no longer our house. We have a guest who does not leave and does not let us sleep. What is mine is his; what is ours is yours, sir. Sovereignty is insolence. Nationalism is pettiness, it is an affront—here in Latin America, for in Europe and Asia the same words have a different meaning.

In the Brasserie La Lorraine in Paris (Place des Ternes), the most powerful elements of tourism foregather. As diplomats speaking Spanish, we dined there one night in 1952. A married couple at a nearby table listened with unusual attention, he with grinning insolence, she elegant and discreet. At last they spoke to us. They were Roumanians who wanted to go to America. In Europe they could no longer "live." War was coming, they affirmed, inevitable, because of Communism. Communism! But the papers were talking about the visit of Tito to England and the royal preparations to receive him. I made this observation warily without a hint of irony. Why is that Communist so welcome? The lady came to the aid of her husband, saying, "It's because Tito professes national Communism." I had in mind, as in a scenario, all the problems I am presenting in this book. It pleased me very much to hear from feminine lips—not always deceitful—a defense of Yugoslav Communists. The husband refused to link up the international with the national. It smelled a bit strange there in the restaurant of live lobsters and roast chicken, *poularde rotie*. But the lady insisted: national Communism, oh yes!

From this one observes that in Europe the word nationalism is still meritorious. Months later, Asia came into the headlines, and Formosa, also commendably nationalist, competed for publicity with the scandal over Guatemala—an infamous nationalism. The European press, also that directed from New York (it was already a Marshallized press), made herculean efforts to prove that Formosa, with 15,000 soldiers on the Pentagon payroll, was the true, the only China—a world power with the right of veto—and that continental China, with ten million square kilometers and 600,000,000 people, was a rachitic, if not fictitious China. The reason for this geographic and demographic topsy-turviness is closer to our understanding, thanks to the Roumanian lady in the Brasserie La Lorraine. Formosa is nationalist! Formosa is something good. Every soldier of Chiang Kai-Shek is worth a thousand of the others. There, in Asia. But here, in Latin America, no; here nationalism is negative, petty; it is treason.

Pause a moment to recall that nationalism had a reactionary origin; for, at the beginning of the modern age, by means of it the aristocracies proliferated and stepped forth to show off their peacock feathers, and bourgeois governments came into power. It is more comforting than amusing to know from the mouth of the Yankee, Flagg Bemis, that the United States as a nation erupted against its neighbors with the banner of "manifest destiny," thanks to its powerful dynamism, which was nationalism. Furthermore, this historian believes that "nationalism is still the most powerful historic force in the entire world."[11] It is comforting and at the same time amusing to know that in 1952 the United Nations recognized the right of all peoples to nationalize their wealth. But what is no longer comforting or amusing, but rather, disconcerting, is to know that the United States does not hesitate to nationalize properties located in its own territory.

Certain western states made deals with private companies to take over their oil—companies who were at the same time the owners of those states. The Senate was the first to observe that petroleum was national wealth. In 1937 the Supreme Court upheld nationalization and the oil was put into the hands of the *Navy*.[12] England herself took a similar step. It was at the end of the war that a

Labor Party government nationalized steel production.

Sure—but we are talking of a world epoch already gone by. Of an epoch in which the fiction of republicans, socialists, liberals, progressives had served as bright beacons in the years of fire. The world was put back in order, and the United States repented. General Dwight Eisenhower took the oil away from the Navy and returned it to the oil men of Texas, of California, of Oklahoma, of Louisiana. The "nationalist" plundering had come to an end. Cinderella Standard Oil got back what was "hers." And the same in England. When the Laborites fell, steel returned to private ownership. "Vickers Cammel Laird" does there what Standard Oil does over here, with advantages so monstrous, so numerous, so overwhelming, that one is deeply saddened. (What in 1950 the State bought for twenty-two million pounds was sold in 1955 to Vickers for ten million. This, without taking into account that the British government had invested twelve millions additional in improvements. What a sweet business! Not so? Read the rest of it in "Europa en America Latina" in *Boletin de la "Agencie Parisienne de Presse,"* March, 1955, No. 3, p. 8.)

England, the United States, and France no longer wished to hear a word about nationalization. That of oil in Iran (1953), of the Suez Canal (1956), the business enterprises in Indonesia (1957), have brought about the demise of many persons and the stripping off of quite a few masks in the international theatre. Masks and men have also fallen in Latin America—Mexico, Argentina, Bolivia—to mention the most painful episodes. The United States has succeeded in creating uniform conformity among the spokesmen who use Spanish. Eudocio Ravines, an old-time

Peruvian Communist who now lives by anti-Kommunism, declares that "nationalism has been converted into the best auxiliary of the Kremlin." [13] [Ravines was exposed as a crypto-Communist—for once this slippery expression seems justified—in 1946 when the Chilean government of Gonzáles Videla broke off relations with the Soviet Union, Jugoslavia, and Czechoslovakia at the behest of the United States and seized official documents, presumably not forged. In these, it was shown that Ravines, Secretary and spokesman for the Conservative landholding party of Peru, was carrying out a Communist assignment which allowed him to pretend not to be Communist and indeed on occasion to attack the Communist Party. After this exposé he became rapidly anti-Communist or, as Arévalo puts it, anti-Kommunist, and thereby became most useful to the State Department—as he still is.—Translator]

Diario Illustrado, a leading daily in Santiago de Chile, editorially commenting on the misfortunes which have overtaken mother England as a result of the loss of Asiatic oil, characterized nationalism as futile, fruitless, and destructive. During the Economic Conference in Buenos Aires (August, 1957), a Colombian delegate said that the "action of nationalist currents" produces mutual jealousy and makes cordiality impossible. And a Brazilian Finance Minister explained, on a certain occasion in New York, that his country suffered from two "financier" diseases; inflation . . . and nationalism, according to *El Mercurio* of August 17, and August 20, 1957.

But let us mount a little higher. The inaugural meeting of the Economic Conference in Buenos Aires was addressed by the president of the nation. He spoke of continental defense and related problems, such as economic stability, and declared that a larger influx of foreign capital was needed. He recalled then the Nazi regimes whose nationalism should not be resuscitated. "Nationalism is a deformation and an exaggeration of patriotism" (*El Mercurio*, August 17, 1957). What a coincidence? England and the United States thought the same! From England we know it even from the mouth of the illustrious Spaniard, Don Salvador de Madariaga, who lives there. On visiting Chile in 1957 he repeated the British opinion that nationalism is negative and merely serves to create barriers against the flow of merchandise (*El Mercurio*, June 22, 1957). We know it also from the United States by many statements and events. Also from the official opinions of the Department of State. Tapley Bennet, head of the Office of South American Affairs, declaimed in our defense: "Ultranationalism is today the principal obstacle obstructing Latin American progress," and he adds, "Ultranationalists and Communists frequently join in tacit cooperation" (*El Mercurio*, July 20, 1954). Treading on his heels—it is an official obligation—comes the Under Secretary of State in charge of Latin American Affairs, Mr. Roy R. Rubottom, in a speech in Miami, January 14, 1958. "Communists utilize nationalism as a Trojan horse." "Communist agents disguise themselves as supernationalists." And he showed us the courtesy of referring to the "nationalist" revolution in Guatemala, which was beheaded in June, 1954. This speech was included in *Documentos y discursos oficiales* (Documents and Official Speeches) published by the Information Service of the United States, Montevideo, January, 1957, 16 pages by mimeograph. (A terrible thing, nationalism must be, when even the Communist parties condemn it. In 1955,

97

the Communist Party of Uruguay expelled from its midst its leader Eugenio Gómez, for "nationalist bourgeois deviation.")

And so all Western Christians have been informed; the new Empire consumes raw materials in *Gargantuan* quantities, and any nationalist attempt to hinder this will be put down as a Kommunist sin. Whatever political tendency or current of ideas or official attitude or legislative project that endangers the draining away of metals for the Metropole or denounces the pyramidal accumulation of profits, or discusses the legality of the treaties and pacts signed by the sardines, will be looked upon as punishable heresy. It is easy to see that we are far beyond the Kommunism and anti-Kommunism of the gendarmes, for whom the sickness consisted of all that attacked the "social institutions," that endangered the fortress of the regime and its permanency in power, anything which dimmed the brilliance of its personality. Political motives and pretexts serve the Police Ruler; commercial motives and pretexts, the North American plutocracy. But man does not live by bread alone, and the imperialist mill utilizes much more than wheat. Alongside nationalism sleeps sovereignty beautiful and trusting, with its end-of-the-century adornments. Sisters in blood, and good sisters. One won't take a step without the other—or they feel unsteady and stumble. Now that nationalism has been stigmatized as evil, the merchants call upon the Pentagon militarists to ridicule and violate sovereignty—the greatest obstacle to military hegemony. The leading historians of our century have not yet agreed whether businessmen give orders to generals (the British view) or whether the generals use the merchants (the German view). The truth is, in all the winding paths

98

of human joy and sorrow, they are seen together, polite to each other, the first providing money, the second giving blows; the one tending the counters, the other burying the dead. Why should the militarists of the United States be insensible to the patriotism of the multimillionaires, who made their fortunes so quickly out of the wealth of others by raising the Yankee flag? Pile up gold, seize the petroleum of the hemisphere, lend money and *hold countries as security*, bribe the Gendarmes, buy a great daily newspaper: does not all this prepare the way, open the ground, for the triumphal entry of the troops?

But there are countries that have not sold out, and dignified governments and rebel university professors and students, and workers, heroic workers, and journalists, who do not have a talent for the feed-bag, and it is against these that the powerful machinery launches its final attack, until they are rounded up into the sheep pen.

Secretary of State John Foster Dulles, whose person combined both military and commercial interests, in April, 1956, made a happy insinuation to the Latin American nations that they renounce a little of their independence and put themselves under the orders of a Special Committee legally domiciled in Washington, according to *El Dia*, Montevideo, April 18, 1956. It was the only way, he said, to arrest the danger of hemispheric Kommunism. But in November, 1957, he went much farther in his proposals for the unity of the twenty-one nations of America and, like any academician, sought support from major historic events. This regent of the Empire explained a bit more about his understanding of the meaning of the unity of the twenty-one nations of America and cited the example of the original thirteen colonies which in 1776 ceased to be thirteen in order to become a single federal entity (*Diario Ilustrado*, November 2, 1957). For years the jurists —English-speaking, Spanish-speaking, Portuguese-speaking —had been talking about interdependence. The shark needs the sardines, the sardines need the shark. If the university professors think this, what can a Police Ruler ask of the legislators waiting for their Cadillac, of the much-decorated journalists, of the "intellectual" who travels about without cost? General Eisenhower, mature in military matters, said once, and Foster Dulles recalled it in his historic November speech: "Nationalist self-sufficiency has gone out of style." Here we have a Christian Dior of politics. In one hand the scissors, over his forearm much cloth to cut, and his mouth full of pins. He decides what still has worth and what has gone out of style. We ourselves would not know if national sovereignty, like individual dignity, could be "out of style." I have heard it said that jealous husbands are out of style, and some of those who say it are also married. And they laugh unconcernedly with placid faces and smooth noble foreheads, doubly noble. It is in this way that the "patriots" laugh at national sovereignty. But not so Eisenhower or Foster Dulles, for they are referring to the national sovereignties of the twenty Republics to the south. The national sovereignty of the United States was never in question, nor will it ever go out of style. The new style or the old style is merely an article of export to Latin America. If there is any sovereign country in the world today, it is precisely the United States. If any country uses its concept of sovereignty more astutely in protecting its own interests, that country is the United States. It is the sovereignty of the small countries which they claim has gone out of style. The weak nations are those "interdependent" *under the crushing imperialist command*. And whoever clamors for defunct sovereignty will do so because he either does not live in this world or is a Kommunist.

Precisely now when science is able to send projectiles to the moon, the United Nations, by the mouth of Leslie Munro, hastens to say that it is urgently necessary to discuss the "sovereignty of the moon and outer space," according to a Reuters dispatch in *El Mercurio* on December 9, 1957.

Yes, already I see them; the Medusa-Cálamo-Serpens making signals from its professional post to make clear to me that in this instance, as in that of the Yankee flag over the South Pole, or that of England over Belice, sovereignty does exist in a subjunctive mood, while that of the twenty nations to the south will be disappearing from the imperative mood. They say that the concept of sovereignty impedes the protection, from outside, of the rights of man, individually conceived. Wherever we turn, human "rights" are becoming the reason—or the pretext—that small nations cannot be independent and survive. The jurists grow lean trying to avoid the difficulties of their logic and do not know how to reconcile contradictory concepts. We empiric politicians, on the other hand, with a bit of good will can see the forest without losing sight of the trees. Perhaps because we know how close at hand the axe is.

I wrote on these questions in *Ensayos Politicos y Discursos*:

> There is no authentic sovereignty in our countries if there has not previously occurred a complete liberation of the human material that comprises the nation.

101

* * *

This internal sovereignty, which is composed of dignity for everybody, is the foundation stone to ward off any danger that may come from outside.

* * *

I have had the conviction—and still have—that a nation cannot be free unless its inhabitants one and all are free, and that the dignity of the Republic is formed by a synthesis of the dignity which is lodged vitally and actively in each one of those who populate its soil.

* * *

For the United States, the anti-imperialism of the Latin Americans is the oldest Kommunist theme. So old that it was born when Mexico was reduced to half its size. The facts are so well known that we shall economize on extensive documentation, which we could put into footnotes. But we will supply some documents so as not to get out of the good habit.

Regarding imperialism, however, we first have to mention concepts which seem blurred because so frequently repeated. There is an imperialism without a flag, which is that practiced by powerful businessmen and bankers in the great cities of both hemispheres and in all periods. This is a world phenomenon, as old as buying and selling, along with the hunchback companion, robbery. The history of this flagless imperialism is the history of commerce, plus the history of banking, plus the history of transportation. A morbid phenomenon, a blemish on economics, is its intimate tie-up with an instinct for usury—an aspect that makes it one of the most sordid chapters of human pathology. Its accidental, or structural, concomitance with things political does not always affect the juridical standards of national life. On the contrary, many states profitably utilize the services of this breed of traders and bankers without a country and do not turn power over to them.

But there is another imperialism that has a nationality, and demands that power be handed over. This imperialism is that of a single state, one single big country, which penetrates into the life of the neighbor carrying and implanting its flag; and with this flag, a few soldiers; and with these soldiers, certain laws. For this political, juridical, and military imperialism, which may or may not have a fundamental economic basis and may or may not continue practicing such ancient and human habits, the essential thing is the taking over of command: the hegemony of the powerful and the subordination of the weak, from the minutest commercial activity to finances, diplomacy, and the army. This imperialism of the flag tosses to one side the concept of a dominant nation being called an Empire, with various tail-tied nations called Dominions, Protectorates, Colonies . . . or Republics.

To combat "imperialism without a flag" is the task of the merchants themselves or resentful competitors or the theoreticians of economy, the sociologists, jurists, and professors of ethics. An anti-imperialism of this sort, so extensive and far-flung, and so humanitarian—an anti-imperialism also without a country—is not the concern of this book. What we call technically anti-imperialism is the battle every citizen should fight against the subordination of the economic, diplomatic, and military interests by a powerful neighbor, whatever may be the pretexts or the falsehoods which the invader may use. We anti-imperialists

103

feel and feed ourselves with passion for our country, our nation! We feel and are fired by the cult of the maternal language, for this language feeds and protects our spirit; we preach sovereignty day and night as a moral exercise, until we come to feel in our souls the beauty of liberty, which is not a myth, but life itself. The anti-imperialism of Latin Americans is made up of these ingredients . . . Kommunists! What are we going to do?

The Peruvian Ravines—again! With the dark leaden pangs of conscience he carries about, and the golden rewards he has contracted for with the "free world," he has told us, "Every anti-imperialist, whatever his nationalist camouflage, is an ally of Communism" (*El Mercurio*, August 27, 1955). And on an earlier occasion, more briefly: "*Communism and anti-Yankeeism* are indistinguishable."[14] It is striking, the loyalty of some Latin Americans for the imperialist language and flag. It is a loyalty of foreign origin, which forces many tasks upon us. But greater still will be these tasks for the Youth of tomorrow when they will have to recover that which we, in this mid-century, did not know how to retain.

NOTES TO CHAPTER III

1. "Intervención," an article signed "Descartes" in the section "Policía y estrategia" of the daily *Democracia* (Buenos Aires), April 30, 1952.

2. "La verdad sobre Gustavo Durán y de la actuación del Hon. Spruille Braden frente a la penetración comunista en las Américas," (The Truth about Gustavo Durán and the Actions of Hon. Spruille Braden toward Communist Penetra-

tion in the Americas). In *Estudios sobre el Comunismo* (Santiago de Chile) , No. 4, 1954, p. 107.

3. *El Mercurio*, October 13, 1957.

4. Cesar Godoy Urrutia, "Hambre y analfabetismo" (Hunger and Illiteracy). In *Educadores del mundo* (Santiago de Chile), No. 10, December, 1957.

5. Betty Kirk, "Los Estados Unidos en la America Latina" (The United States in Latin America). In *Cuadernos Americanos* (México) January-February, 1958, p. 9.

6. Harvey O'Connor, *El imperio del petróleo* (Oil Empire) (México, 1956), p. 151.

7. Brady, pp. 302-3.

8. Carlos Davila, "Ciento cincuenta años de lucha obrera en los Estados Unidos" (One Hundred and Fifty Years of Labor Struggle in the United States) *Revista América* (Havana) , September, 1945.

9. Seldes, *Mil Norteamericanos: los dictadores de los Estados Unidos*, 1st ed., pp. 58ff.

10. "Nuevo Frente Comunista en Argentina: organización del Congreso por la Cultura" (New Communist Front in Argentina: Organization of the Congreso por la Cultura). In *Estudios sobre el Comunismo* (Santiago de Chile), No. 6, 1954, pp. 59ff.

11. Carlos Ibarguren, *De Monroe a la Buena Vecindad* (From Monroe to the Good Neighbor) (Buenos Aires, 1946), p. 112.

12. O'Connor, on various pages; Raúl Osegueda, *Operación Centroamérica O.K.* (Operation Central America O.K.) (México, 1957) , pp. 71, 77.

13. "La Estrategia Comunista en América Latina" (The Communist Strategy in Latin America). In *Estudios sobre el Comunismo* (Santiago de Chile), No. 6, 1954, pp. 70ff.

14. *Ibid.*, p. 71.

IV.

THE CATHOLIC CHURCH
AND ITS
ANTI-KOMMUNISM

Religion which allies itself with injustice against the natural aspirations
of the masses is worse than atheism.
                    —Henry George

We shall save the world by giving
bread to those who are hungry or we
shall perish under the crushing weight
of the gold accumulated at the price
of the hunger and misery of two-
thirds of our fellow beings.
                    —Josué de Castro

Just as a few pages back we jumped from the catacombs
of the Caribbean to those of the banks of New York in
order to follow the capricious trajectory of the word Kommunism, once more we must prove how agile we are by
jumping from the basements of a skyscraper to the dome
of St. Peter, with the purpose of finding out what the
Catholic Church understands by Kommunism. If the leap

which carried us from the obscure conscience of the Police Ruler to the equally obscure conscience of the international English-speaking usurers was as audacious and spectacular as the brave stunt of a tightrope walker, audacious and spectacular also will be our trapeze flight from the world of those who are almost illiterate to the world of philosophy; from the world of those who do not know what to do with the mountains of dead bodies and the money of their neighbors, to the world that analyzes texts in Hebrew, in Greek, and in Latin and meditates and meditates all night on the mystery of life to try to explain it in terms of living and to show men of good will the road toward the kingdom of God.

If the Police-State Rulers and the Caudillos of Business, the Robber Barons, are there hunched on the banks of the great river of culture to watch the waves and foam pass by, amused by their own importance and their fawning hangers-on, the representatives of the Catholic Church cannot be seen anywhere on the bank, for they are in the river itself: they are culture, knowledge, and the illuminated life. We pass, therefore, from the world of the ignorant to the world of wise men, probably more enlightened than those who walk elbow to elbow with us. For the Catholic Church is the mother of wisdom. It is not built on a thick stone dragged out of the nearest quarry; it is brought forth from the doctrine of Christ the philosopher, the socialist, the revolutionist, the rebel, the transformer, He of the sublime words and exemplary life. But when it established itself, and organized itself to endure through the centuries, the Church went even further than Jesus of Galilee. It drank then of the materialism of the Hebrews; what it needed in the way of idealism it extracted from

107

Plato and Plotinus; and when *realism* became necessary, it took as its own the best of Aristotle, and if the *moral* was need for its adornment, there were the stoics bringing their treasure and the Pythagoreans, theirs; and in social material the Churchmen appropriated the Communism of the Essenes; and they took what they could from the Pharisees, nor did they disdain the practices and the rites of paganism. Centuries later appeared the indispensable geniuses to bring order to this plurality of theories, this jostling promiscuity: Saint Augustine of Africa and Saint Thomas Aquinas.

Therefore, when from a Peréz Jiménez, a Batista, and a Somoza, or a McCarthy, a Braden, or a Rockefeller, we plunge breathlessly into the world of Savonarola, of Borromeo, of Newman, of Consalvi; into the world of San Ignacio de Loyola, and Leo XIII, we are venturing with the same sort of audacity which characterized the fifteenth-century navigators, who crossed the ocean to settle in worlds different from their own. [Peréz Jiménez, recent dictator of Venezuela, later jailed in Miami. The Somozas, dictators of Nicaragua whose power was derived from the U.S. Marine invasion. Archbishop Carlos Borromeo of Milan, noted for his erudition and his fearless abnegation during the 1583-84 plague. San Ignacio de Loyola, founder of the Jesuit order and hence the Inquisition. Leo XIII, a Pope famous for his Labor encyclicals deemed very revolutionary when first issued. Cardinal Hercules Consalvi (1757-1824) Minister of Pope Pius VII, negotiated the Concordat with Napoleon.—Translator]

In short, no one can say that the Catholic Church walks in the shadows or over rough hidden paths. It has the *cosmography* which the Police Rulers and the loan merchants of New York do not have. Better said, it has a lofty doctrine of knowledge and learning. Even so, there is also a philosophy inherent in the conduct of a Police Ruler and the Superintendent of Enterprise. But theirs is a philosophy made with the feet, as Ortega y Gasset ironically suggested; it is a philosophy of living merely to live, and to live in this way and keep on living does require a philosophy, one so natural, so spontaneous, that intelligence is not involved, something so smooth and impalpable that it springs from the mere act of walking or masticating food. It is a philosophy which serves for such purposes; to walk and to masticate, to trot up and down the roads, including those of others; to chew the cud of all meals, including those of others. It is to a certain extent peripatetic, in a certain way diuretic, with the echo of neighs and kicks, a long elastic lope, straight to the table. It is a philosophy that a pure-bred horse would have if he could speak or could read and write.

We cannot say such things about the Catholic Church. It has an audacious concept of the world though, like most great concepts, it is rubbed down by diverse antagonistic and alien elements. This philosophy instead of hoofs has wings. It is high meditation about what is lofty. It is a philosophy of values, which tries to show us the road to perfection and salvation. Here the techniques of mastication and salvation, of peptonic chemistry, do not intrude. Catholic philosophy seeks in man what is man, not what remains of the animal. It gives specific advice on how to get rid of the feed-bag and travel over spiritual highways to that world which is offered to us by the word Heaven, there to meet God. Be this real or merely symbolism, it deals with a standard of conduct, a program worthy of the human being, a hope. A man purely man is not interested in perfection; he is content with perfecting himself.

Naturally this superior doctrine of values which animates Catholic theory is not an empty philosophy: it is a functioning religious philosophy; it is religion. It is a world of ideas which are not reached by tenacious study by the light of day or in the night's peace, not an achievement or a gain in human intelligence. This philosophy of Catholicism is made primarily through Revelation. To reach it, we do not walk on tiptoes nor get hold of stilts; it is reached, according to the apostles, because it was the word of God which descended even unto man. The truth is, it was handed to us as a gift, and out of that gift we created dogmas. This Revelation, this free gift from a celestial treasury, came to earth with the preaching of Jesus, as collected later in the Evangels, on the word of honor of Luke, Paul, Mark, John, and Matthew.

A philosophy thus derived from on high, a divine legacy, can be commented upon but not argued about. To argue about it, we must be as much god as God, and that cannot be accepted. For this reason the philosophy of the Catholic Church is received, is admitted, is lodged in the conscience of the believer and becomes conduct. It is an operational philosophy, but it is also an imperative. Those who follow it are believers; those who argue about it are reprobates.

From this very intimate modality sprouted the struggle of the Church with its surrounding world: a struggle of centuries, written with the blood of millions, that started on the hill of Golgotha, continued as a circus spectacle in the Rome of the Caesars, and was projected across the deserts; that burned cities, unleashed militant warriors,

110

crossed the seas, subjugated nations of nonbelievers, erecting gallows and combining confession with tortures. It administered the god of the saints and purified sinners with the help of fire. In this way, the Catholic Church, besides its conception of the world, had a psychology of expansion and pugnacity: a history of centuries-old Cyclopean battle, which set in motion the passions of mankind, from noble passions to the fermentation of the dregs. It fought with the Hebrew sects, with Greek-Roman paganism, even with the military Empire—and captured it. The Church endured the Saracen avalanche, confronted the Protestant heterodoxy in all its shadowy and its militant phases, returned to the battle to fight the Emperors of the West and also to fight the Italian people themselves, until, step by step, it lost the City of Rome. Such is the history, more or less superficial, which we learned in school and from outside texts.

But the books we were not told about, and which we were obliged to read without ecclesiastical license and without scholarly assistance, gave us another history, the internal history of the Papacy, that of the governing bodies of high ecclesiastics and the priesthood, in which the contenders were theory versus practice, faith versus temperament, advice for others versus the conduct of the advisers themselves. Popes, Cardinals, Archbishops, Sacerdotes had to arrange their lives according to the precepts laid down. This was a more important and difficult conflict. For the political and military history of the Church against its outside adversaries was nothing but a struggle for vital living space, and for that it could count on the multitude of faithful who had been brought by millions under the spell of Christ. But this other struggle, for cleanliness of

111

conduct and loyalty to the doctrine contained the threat of a crack-up, of internal disintegration which causes believers to lose their faith, to fly toward other sects; the death of the Church without even fighting outside enemies, without thunder or bloodshed.

We do not miss the opportunity of mentioning that it was not the simple priests but the Popes themselves who failed to observe the established principles, made spectacles of themselves in public, and covered the Church with shame. John XIII had his throat cut in San Angelo Castle, and Boniface VII, one of the accomplices of that crime, ascended the throne of St. Peter. People said Sylvester VII had a pact with the devil: such was his life. Stephen VI had the bodies of his predecessors dug up, their fingers cut off, and then dragged through the streets of Rome. John XIX became Pope through the money of his family. Benedict IX sold his high position to the one who could pay the most: Gregory VI.

Another Pope, of the Borgia family, made his son, Cesare, the most beautiful assassin in the Italy of those days, a Cardinal. Pope John VIII died from a hammer blow dealt him by a relative who wanted to be Pope, after this same pious and persistent relative had failed in a poison attempt. It is known that Clement V was a libertine and corrupt in the management of Christianity's funds, to such an extent the banks denied him credit. Pope Sixtus IV, better to steal money, invented a crusade against the Turks. Leo X considered the papacy to be his personal property, to the extent that every other minute he repeated, "We enjoy the papacy, because God gave it to us."[1]

These, reader, are only a few bits taken at random here and there from the internal history of the Church. If

Popes and Cardinals and priests refused to follow faithfully the severe moral line of Catholicism and deformed the fundamental precepts, the Church itself was exposed to danger. Nevertheless, the assassinations "en familia," the theft of sacred funds, the bribery and dishonesty, the sexual intercourse, the personal enrichment, and other forms of corruption did not succeed in destroying the foundations of the institution. The Church rose above itself, and the papacy was elevated despite such sinister figures. In spite of the blood, the money, the sexual licentiousness, *a moral doctrine* shone intact. All the sensual indulgences, all the hypocrisies, all the apostasies remained extracurricular. Life as it is enjoyed, enjoyment as a sport, could not be permitted inside the great cathedral.

In our days the Church seems sufficiently alleviated from such painful afflictions. (However, the death of Pope Pius XII caused universal murmuring against Vatican customs. Apparently the business of business was more important than spiritual business. The relatives of the Pope, after twenty years with "free opportunities," are now among the chief millionaires of Italy. The inhabitants of Rome at this writing have food only for a few months. On this side of the Atlantic the matter is of no importance.) Mussolini helped the Church recuperate, when, as some express it, the institution was prostrate in bed. Convalescing, it was able to obtain advantages from Nazism, through bishops and archbishops allied with Hitler. General Franco, the most generous of all, gave everything, even part of his power. Moreover, in the hours of the second world conflagration, the Vatican had a great pilot, this same Pius XII, friend of Roosevelt, who worked out an alliance, this time with the Western powers. Since the war, the Catholic Church has enjoyed the best of health. Without relinquishing its privileges in Madrid, it has made an alliance with the United States. It has not been necessary for either side to define this. The Church is interested in what belongs to it—eternity—and its experience over painful centuries has made it suspicious. As an ancient fighter against revolutionary doctrines, it has sought and obtained the friendship of the powerful. The Empires on their side need it. The imperialists, too, are tired of social convulsions and political experiments. The struggle against Kommunism now provides the pretext for their alliance. Thus, the Great protect themselves mutually against the pressures of the masses.

Here we have the reason why, in our task of tracking down what is meant in Latin America by Kommunism, we have not been able to close our ears to the voice of the Catholic Church. Naturally it has its own motives. We are not going to insist that its calculations coincide with those of the police of Paraguay or with those of United Fruit. The root source of its calculations is different and, for this reason, very serious, the consequences decidedly dramatic —even more so for Latin America, since in these confused moments, a mysterious social and political development is taking place. Nobody, whether suffering or fortunate, can deny that the twenty Latin countries are being served up in the soup to test out the most unusual ideological combinations. The Catholic Church, among us since 1492, is participating in the laboratory hardships. With what intentions? For what profit? This we can find out by descending to the field of battle.

The Catholic clergy also has its representative personages. If the Latin American democracies have their significant Colonel Lazo, and if the merchants of the free world exhibit their Spruille Braden, Latin American Catholicism has its Mariano Rossell y Arellano, Archbishop of Guatemala. These are symbolic men, they are archetypes. An Antillean General, we have observed, has been genial enough to augment the wages of corpses, the plump Yankee millionaire was about to die of hunger at the end of a banquet. We shall learn even more marvelous things about Rossell y Arellano.

Mariano Rossell y Arellano has the lean figure of those sacerdotes who neither eat nor sleep in order to take care of their generous aristocratic clientele which frequents the sacristies and attends Sunday Mass. Well built and circumspect, slow of pace, with studied gestures, his robes immaculate, this sacerdote of San Sebastián came to be Archbishop through the help of the strong arm of President Ubico. That government, as we know, was the prototype of Police Rule. Ubico said he belonged to the Liberal Party, an adversary of the Church, but which serves the Church and its sacerdotes. Rulers who pile up crimes in the lowest depths of their conscience are usually more anxious than anybody else for the help of someone who will exculpate them. Ubico more than anybody else needed this help. He enjoyed the friendship of Papal nuncios, bishops, and prelates. When the post of Archbishop fell vacant, Ubico's excellent relations with the Vatican enabled him to suggest that the position be given to the priest Rossell y Arellano. The Holy See acceded to the wishes of this exemplary Ruler.

Since then, Rossell y Arellano's gratitude toward his protector and godfather has been boundless. I will not say that he put the altars at the feet of the tyrant, but the

115

Catholic Church in Guatemala, its priests, and its bishops —so long as the people supported the bloody dictatorship of fourteen years—did not open their mouths. But those "legitimate successors of the apostles, chosen by the Holy ghost to govern the Church of God," had no ears for the groans of those tortured in the Central Penitentiary nor did they give extreme unction to Catholics who died on the highways, assassinated by the government on the excuse that they tried to escape (Ley de Fuga). Two thousand five hundred Guatemalan Catholics perished under the Rule of the Generalissimo—the same one who was given fantastic money gifts by the Legislative Assembly.

The Canadian writer, William Krehm, on page 85 of his widely distributed book, *Democracia y Tiranías en el Caribe,* published in Mexico in 1949, charges that in merely two days, Ubico ordered three hundred Catholic Guatemalans shot. [Krehm would not tailor his news—he was *Time* correspondent—to suit the propaganda purposes of the U.S. Embassy and was denied even a transit visa to return to Canada. Eventually he lost his job.—Translator]

Gregorio Selser and Vicente Sáenz provide an additional document: Monseñor Canuto Reyes y Valladares, Bishop of Granada, in February, 1927, blessed the arms of a battalion of (Protestant) North Americans, who had come to that country [Nicaragua] to murder Nicaraguan Catholics. From the pulpit he had excommunicated those fighting with Sandino. The Yankees, on passing through the town of Yalí, looted and wrecked the church, and among other things, stole the gold censer. When the Yankee battalion was wiped out by the patriots, Sandino—Catholic and . . . Kommunist—returned the censer to the priests. (Gregorio Selser: *Sandino, General de los Hombres Libres,* Buenos

116

Aires, 1959, Vol. 1, p. 180; Vol. II, p. 21.) [Yali is in north-west Nicaragua near the Honduras frontier. Granada is the conservative city at the northwest end of Lake Nicaragua.—Translator]

Undeniably the blame for these crimes, in spite of their having been committed in conformity with a presidential political plan, does not fall wholly on the person of the President. He had ardent collaborators, all of them inspired by the example of "their commander," when as a mere Jefe politico in Retalhuleu (1911-19), he murdered Mexicans and "thieves" for no good reason. It is thus that administrative collaborators pass from apprenticeship to proficiency in the task of [destroying] human flesh. [Retalhuleu is a large center and province in southwest Guatemala near the Pacific. Coffee, sugar, and cattle are major products.—Translator]

All these are descendants of the founders of the country. Naturally none of these founded a city or a town, or a village; but they did found cemeteries. (Frederick II of Germany [around 1220] also complained of not having enough space in which to bury his enemies.) Thus Ubico set up his experienced team and thus he headed the government for fourteen years. Rossell y Arellano knew about everything, as did everybody in the little country. Nevertheless, when the Police Ruler had to flee terrified before unleashed popular wrath, the Pastor of the Catholic flock, addressing the whole nation, called the fugitive assassin "a good man."

Note how gentle is the verbal expression, how in keeping with the delicate silken quality of the Señor Archbishop. Good man, bad man are not explosive designations and serve neither to consecrate nor to bury. Any

117

passerby can repeat them, and nobody will pay especial attention to what was said. But when the phrase emanates from one who is speaking "in the name of the Holy Apostolic See" and with "the authority of God" conferred on him, the word takes on significance and weight and purpose. And if such a Church dignitary utters such simple words, applying them to the individual who ordered the assassination of two thousand Catholics, the matter takes on more serious proportions. For the philosophy inherent in Christian doctrine obliges its spokesmen to weigh words carefully and respect them. Who is a good man and who is a bad man, an Archbishop should know with scientific certainty. An Archbishop is a grade higher than Colonel Lazo or a manufacturer of automobiles. But an Archbishop —still in office—called Jorge Ubico "a good man."

Regarding the religious and humane sentiments of this "good man," his psychology, and his morals, read at least these two works: *Leifugados* by Carlos Alberto Sandoval (Mexico, 1946), and *Ombres contra Hombres* by Efrain de los Rios (Guatemala, 1948, 2 vols., Second edition). [The first edition, Mexico, 1945, is in one volume. It is a hair-raising account of persecutions, torture, and murders, also a damning exposé of the shameful conduct of the U.S. Ambassador and his relations to the dictatorship and to prisoners.—Translator]

"A dignified and worthy ruler of Central America" was Somoza, according to priest Mario Casariegos of San Salvador. He said so over the radio in early June, 1954, only eight years after the adjective "good" had been applied to the reaper of human lives and the despoiler of the properties of others. Now the word "good" is no longer enough to exalt the conduct of a good neighbor of the same stripe.

Now it is necessary to resort to the word "dignity." We insist on our protest. The doctrine of Christ which has held aloft incarnate through all the centuries considered that the ultimate essence of the human being was the concept of *dignity*. That, it is said, is what in nature distinguishes man from the brutes. The entire theory of personality lives in the words of the Nazarene; and Christian ethic (stoicism, platonism, Aristotelianism joined together) develops these ideas with incomparable mastery. Therein "dignity" flames like an ensign, as if to tell each and all of us that we possess a trace of what is superior. Did not God make us in his own image?

But if just around the corner, we are told that the divinity in human beings shines most dazzlingly in men such as Somoza and such as Ubico, we are struck by the deep fear that we do not properly understand these modern sacerdotes, that again we will surprise them contradicting the teachings of Christ. We cannot admit, in short, that a priest or an Archbishop can overthrow the concept of the good and of dignity in order to use such words as pedestals for the assassins in power. But is it merely the assassins?

Something has just struck our imagination, with the fleetness of a swift swallow which, darting, hesitating, trying to escape, crossed before our eyes one twilight when the horizon was most serene and luminous. And this is that for history Ubico and Somoza (and the Church too?) have *one thing in common* besides their police forces, besides the blood of Catholic compatriots smeared on the Generalissimos' much adorned uniforms, besides their repeated violations of civil law and moral law. It has something to do with whatever it is that makes them "good"

119

and "worthy" in the eyes of foreigners, in the eyes of exporters and importers, as well as in those neo-Catholic sacerdotes of Guatemala and San Salvador. And as the idea cleaves the air like a swallow and disturbs our meditation, we read in the recent book of Raúl Osegueda. There on page 56, Raúl informs us that in 1927 the Bishop of Managua invoked the protection of God in behalf of the ruler Adolfo Díaz. Who is and whence came this heaven-protected Adolfo Díaz? You, reader, and I know. The Catholic Church also knows. Adolfo Díaz is the man whom the United States utilized when it tried to "buy" a republic of Central America for three million dollars. (This matter is more fully discussed in my book, *The Shark and the Sardines* [New York: Lyle Stuart, 1961].) This is the man they made use of. . . . Zas! The small swallow again. This pragmatic instrumentalized blend of utility with truth, of men of means and presidents as lackeys: this obsession of the practical, of the "possible," this English idea of the "goal" and the "record," this international diplomacy of fictitious but useful governments, so similar to the detours within Christianity toward a fictitious but useful clergy—nothing more is needed to explain the fraternity of the Somozas, the Ubicos, the Díazes, and the uniformity with which they are admired by priests and Archbishops.

Unfortunately in this chapter we cannot untie the conceptual knots with the same facility as when we laughed at the Police Rulers and the Knights of Industry. We are now in the field of the scholastic, and we do not have any excuse to jump over the problems. For in the theme we are facing, it is the Catholic Church that is laughing at us. From the twelfth to the thirteenth century, when a number of Popes enjoyed themselves by wallowing in sensuality and vice, or enriched themselves so munificently or cut each other's throats better to serve God, the Church invalidated reproaches by reminding the ignorant that within Christianity the human person is free and for this very reason, a sinner, hence a matter for earthly inquisition and for judgment after death. A Pope is not the papacy, nor even are twenty Popes. The Archbishops and Sacerdotes can commit simony, as can any lay Catholic err without the Church sharing the guilt. Individual opinion and private conduct are concealed where no police can ferret them out. The Church acts on these premises, and for it the conduct of each person has its own accounting. To classify one man good and another a worthy governor, just as invoking the protection of God for a third, were personal concerns of an Archbishop, the Sacerdote, the Bishop. Why must the Church be involved in these petty matters?

The swallow returns to break through the flimsiness of these excuses, to oblige me to recall the death of Somoza in 1956, at which time the State and the Empire stood together. A suicidal patriot killed "the owner" of his country, and did so without ecclesiastical permission and without any insinuations from the Empire. A Protestant voice from Washington called Rigoberto López Pérez "a cowardly assassin." Without doubt a philosophical nicety, a distortion of language. To call a man a coward who risks his life because he believes he is serving his country is a new way of speaking. Señor Eisenhower was unconsolable. The free world was unconsolable. Anastasio the Great had died. Months later in the United States, a subject named Anastasia had his throat cut. Naturally this individual did not enjoy friendship with the President; he

121

had it only with the Vice-Lords and the Sub-Caesars. But the Protestant Empire is not alone. There at its side stands the Catholic Church. And the Catholic authorities ordered that Anastasio Somoza be buried with the honors of a Prince of the Church. Such honors were an apotheosis granted to Roman Caesars and put the defunct person in the category of "savior" and "liberator." They preserve him from the dangers of decomposition and carry him "beyond death." [2] Anastasio Somoza, blessed is thy name! When we heard it we lifted our head humbly to gaze on high, to that which the traditional grandmother and the modern mother have taught us to respect. And we merely asked in low voice, "But why, Señor, why? It appears that we are on the way to canonize these political beasts of the Caribbean, who, the more blood they spill the more they become Princes—and more Catholic."

But in Guatemala there died in a similar manner another Police Ruler. [This refers to Castillo Armas, a petty dictator imposed in 1954 on the Guatemalan people by paid mercenaries, with arms furnished by the C.I.A. and the Pentagon, and the dutiful aid of the other Central American rulers, in violation of all international law. He was assassinated a year or so later.—Translator] For him to be the Ruler, the aid of five foreign governments and the pastoral letters of Archbishop Rossell y Arellano were indispensable. The United Fruit Company, an enterprise that grows and exports bananas, wished to recover certain idle lands that had been confiscated, and refused to pay various millions of dollars owed the national treasury, and it wished to recover political control over the nation which it had lost since 1944, and it needed. . . . Very well! To please it, various pastorals were pronounced ordering the faithful to "obey the mandates of the Church, which commands us to fight and destroy the forces of Communism." A colonel for hire, ready for anything, appeared, and Archbishop Rossell y Arellano put him under the protection of God and the Christ of Esquipulas. [This is a miraculous image worshipped in the town of Esquipulas, near the Honduras frontier.—Translator] But neither God nor the miraculous Christ accepted the guardianship of a man who produced five hundred cadavers of Guatemalan Catholics in three years; and they permitted Castillo Armas to be killed by his intimate friends in his own house, with the same arms they had brought from abroad. Again the world displayed consternation. Again the telegrams and the adjectives of the Emperor. Rossell y Arellano, who happened to be *in Rome,* hastened his return to Guatemala and arrived (Oh, swallow in the peaceful evening!) in a North American military plane accompanied by Eisenhower's son, the Crown Prince. Why a "Roman" priest in a military airplane? The pair came direct from Washington. The truth is that the two (one Catholic, the other Protestant) arrived in time for the burial rites of the Liberator of United Fruit. And it was there that Rossell y Arellano dared lift his oratorical fire far beyond what is licit, saying that Castillo Armas had been as good as Jesus Christ. According to a United Press dispatch to *La Nación* of Santiago de Chile on July 13, 1957, he compared Castillo Armas' policy of kindness (!) to the kindness for which Jesus Christ was sacrificed.

Do you see, Reader? Once again the personal opinion, the liberty of the individual judgment, the possibility of falling into sin, be it verbal irresponsibility or simony. But can an Archbishop compare a political delinquent to

Jesus Christ with impunity? (Charlemagne in his reprimands to Pope Leo III ordered him to devote himself "most diligently in uprooting the heresy of simony which in many holy places besmirched the sacred body of the Church." As we readily see, the evil is very ancient. The ultra-Catholic adversaries of that Pope, according to the same source, accused him of "adultery and perjury.")

That the Castillo Armas government had *burned books* (even those of Sarmiento and Victor Hugo) in the public plaza is not surprising, because the Saracens and the Christians had done so during a war of life and death against heterodoxy and did so again in Spain in 1939. [Domingo Sarmiento, the great cavalier President of Argentina, who reestablished civil rights, founded the country's free public school system and opened up the Pampa to settlement, was also the author of some sixty books, including the novel *Facundo*, considered one of the great classics. *Facundo* was a devastating picture of the ignorant gaucho dictator, his brutalities and crimes. It was probably, too, devastatingly similar to the ignorant strutting alcoholic protege of the C.I.A. and the State Department.—Translator] Neither does it surprise us that Castillo Armas *burned the bodies* of Catholic peasants, because fire was used by the Holy Mother Church to purify the bodies of those who deviated from the route traced by her to be followed. But to these police and institutional methods, which never found a place in the good soul of Jesus, Castillo Armas added others which likewise would have been condemned by Jesus. He *received money* from the United Fruit to simulate a revolution (five million dollars according to Castillo Armas' own confession to a Cuban journalist [*Bohemia,* November 28, 1954]. A Guatemalan

124

journalist, a Catholic and an admirer of Castillo Armas, has said that the total received at that time was six million.) He *received arms* from a foreign power to kill fellow-citizens, received donations from the State Department that totaled 60 million dollars, received gifts in money (25,000 dollars) from a commercial firm which Castillo Armas had permitted to raise the prices of prime necessities at that moment very scarce, received. . . . What didn't he get? But if these are the "Catholic" antecedents of Castillo Armas, the Archbishop could not have dared to compare him with Jesus Christ. In any case, he could have been compared to Cardinal Cesare Borgia. Yes, and to many who like him revealed a psychology and a morality . . . of the Renaissance. Does it not seem, Monseñor, that you went to extremes in your desire to please United Fruit and the Eisenhower family?

* * *

At this point we close our presentation of our personage. We have extended ourselves a bit on the theme, not because it dealt with Central American political documentation, but because Monseñor Rossell y Arellano provides us with even more important documents useful for our investigation of what we should understand by anti-Kommunism.

From an ideological standpoint, the most striking aspect of our observations, when we dissected the Knights of Industry of New York, was the recognizing that all identified Socialism, be it Marxist or not, be it Christian or not, with Communism. A Catholic Church dignitary who has taken courses in sociology and metaphysics, who has received credits in Latin and has been a diplomat in Rome, cannot err by being naive. The Knights of Industry are men with only a rudimentary culture and any illiterate can confuse Socialism with Communism. Rossell y Arellano, however, goes even further than the barbarians in his conceptual confusions. For him Kommunism cannot be distinguished from liberalism and conservatism. At the start, he said, "Economic liberalism and conservatism lead to Communism." [3] On July 21, 1954, hundreds of faithful gathered in front of the Archbishop's palace in Guatemala to celebrate his birthday; they applauded him enthusiastically for the liberation of United Fruit.

In order to keep his hand in, the Archbishop made another political address.[4] "My beloved sons," he began. And at once added: Communism is only the third act of the great process of which the first two are liberalism and conservatism. It is impossible to put an end to it, unless the first two are abolished. Liberalism and conservatism carry the same disease germ: the fundamental principle of Communism: atheistic laws. So long as there are atheistic laws there will be Communism. For the orator on his birthday, the Communist problem reduced itself to a problem of God. The kernel of Communism was in the negation of God. Of God and the Fatherland. He had said, ever since his April 4, 1954, pastoral: "The people of Guatemala should rise up as one man against the enemy of God and the Fatherland."[5]

The docile sheep naturally identified the Guatemalan government with the enemy of God and the Fatherland. Rise up against the constitutional government, "rise up as one man," is an incitement usually heard in the mouth of social agitators, of demagogic leaders, but never in the

126

mouth of a spokesman of Christ. Above all when we know that the revolutionary governments of Guatemala, from October 20, 1944 on, had never done anything against the Catholic Church, the religion of the majority of Guatemalans, or against the resident priests or against the customs and observances of Catholic believers. The sole "crime" was that of having legislated in favor of the workers (1947) and agrarian reform (1952), which seriously affected the profit orgies of United Fruit. This is why the Archbishop's voice found no echo whatever among the Catholics of the country, who remained indifferent to his pastorals and his lying tears. Real tears, in contrast, were those of Foster Dulles and of Eisenhower, who glued themselves to the microphone, weeks after the Archbishop, also to invite the Guatemalans to "rise as one man" against the enemies of the Empire and freedom of opportunity.

In that 1954 pastoral, Rossell y Arellano had repeated very serious words about the Fatherland: "Communism is atheism and atheism is antipatriotic." Any policeman, any Knight of Industry, is startled and moved. Is it possible that the fate of God is endangered along with a country called Guatemala, or by that other fatherland called United Fruit? No; this is not what is at stake. Rossell y Arellano has committed another sin. It does not concern the simony, the corruption—as this was—of putting the Catholic Church at the service of an enterprise of colonial merchants; it concerns the bad faith displayed in confusing the intelligence of the faithful by means of a play on words, a play of phrases. Rossell y Arellano should have explained that he was using the word Fatherland or Patria as it is used by all the sacerdotes of the Catholic world, as it is understood in theology. "The road that Christ points out leads where all roads end, the place where no other starts, to the presence of the Father, to the Patria, hence is that for which the heart of every pilgrim on earth sighs." [6]

Do you see it now, my Reader? With what simplicity and with what doctrinaire loyalty the theologians of our day, as in all eras, tell us that the Fatherland, the Patria is in God, for God is the redeemer, the refuge, the harbor where on arrival worries and longings are no longer. On other occasions, we are told that the Fatherland is Heaven; but Heaven in theology is nothing more than man's encounter with God. There is no way, therefore, to lose oneself. The concept of Fatherland in the mouths of priests is a theological concept, and this concept has nothing to do with the civic, juridical, psychological, political, historic, or social concept of the word "Patria" which we use in our earthly, sinful, mundane existence prior to our encounter with God.

The negation of God as a metaphysical entity, and not merely as the supreme religious value, is called atheism. The Catholic Church, as does any religion whatever, combats and punishes atheism, opposes all the doctrines, religious or not, which deny the reality of God. I do not know if all Communists are atheists; I do not know if the liberals and conservatives are atheists; but if they were, if their doctrines in themselves presupposed the negation of God, then true enough Communism, liberalism, and conservatism would be anti-patriotic in the theological sense that they deny God, which for theologians is the fatherland. Agreed then, Señor Archbishop, that if God is Fatherland, atheism is anti-patriotic. But what we cannot admit is that you deny to the Catholics of Guatemala these elementary explanations, and that you have utilized muddy and equivocal notions to accelerate and facilitate the return of the United Fruit to the presidential office in Guatemala, and thereby made enslavement of three million Catholic workers easier and more prolonged.

Thorstein Veblen observed in his *Theory of the Leisure Class* that of all the despicable things that exist, the most despicable is the man who appears as a sacerdote of God and is the sacerdote of his own comfort and ambitions.

* * *

We are now, dear Reader, a whole ocean nearer: a voyage, if not calm, not especially audacious. We have left behind the continent of Socialist ideas, tendencies and laws, the Socialist or socializing parties, and we step ashore on a new continent: liberalism, which we never believed would be tainted by Communism. But the Archbishop of Guatemala has pointed an accusing finger at liberalism not only as an antecedent of Communism, but has tried also to make it over into the cause of Communism. Elemental logic teaches us that not all antecedents can be considered to be causes. The Communist doctrine of the Church Fathers, such as Tertulian, Saint Ambrose, Saint Cyprian, Gregory of Nacianceno, for instance, honorable precursors in the trajectory of human thought cannot be considered as the cause of anti-Kommunism which certain Catholic clergymen profess in our day. The doctrine of Jesus himself, which has been transmitted to us in didactic formulas or in evangelical texts, as a socialist and revolutionary doctrine, a defense of the humble and the enemy of the rich, cannot in any way, not even by dragging it in

129

by the hair, be advanced as a cause of the actual alliance between the Falangist clergy and the North American millionaires.

"It is easier for a camel to pass through the eye of a needle, than for a rich man to enter the kingdom of heaven," Jesus would say, an observation the sacerdotes of our day take pains to forget. In fact, Rossell y Arellano himself in the previously mentioned 1954 pastoral letter insisted on justifying excessive riches, telling of the "inequality of goods, which will always exist as a consequence of the original sin."

Clearly the history of Christianity sets forth contradictions that cannot be bridged. A contradiction, for example, into which Rossell y Arellano falls, in theoretically and verbally condemning "economic liberalism" in the same breath that he personally endeavors to help a commercial enterprise recover its political dominion over the Guatemalan nation. For does it not so happen that all this grandiose iron ring of companies, enterprises, and banks with headquarters in New York, is the product of economic liberalism? And is not liberalism, English liberalism, the philosophy of the United States? And is not the United Fruit one of the important suction pumps seated in the Department of State itself? Rossell y Arellano is not ignorant of this. How, then, is it possible for him to fight liberalism as a philosophic "cause" and at the same time permit it to enter the house as a commercial "effect?" If liberalism is the cause of Kommunism, does this not mean that the "freedom of opportunity" predicated by the Department of State is thereby Kommunism?

Obviously we have exaggerated the argument. We are proceeding like those persons who wish to get a rational, satisfactory, irreproachable explanation for every problem in life. Actually we don't belong to that species. So again we must admit that human life is full of contrary meanings, and one of these contradictions is that between expressed ideas and actual conduct. The Falangist Catholic clergy take advantage of this traditional dichotomy. They are associated with the United States as human beings and march along with it side by side, creating their own commercial and political strength, and both have made a pact of life and death against Kommunism even though the theory of liberalism separates them. We recognize, we also, the "right" they have of not providing explanations. In the last analysis the United States doesn't give them either. It is fundamentally a Protestant nation. Is it possible that Protestantism and Catholicism, as great branches of Christianity, have joined to fight Kommunism? We shall soon observe that no religious pact is involved. That colossal religious rupture which carried to this side of the Atlantic a few Pilgrims who fled from intolerance and sought a country where they could love Christ with liberty of conscience—that rupture is still maintained.

"From its first days, the Catholic Church repudiated freedom of thought, taking this to mean freedom of all opinions and considering this to be the gravest of all sins." This is stated by a great Catholic theologian.[7] The truth is, no religion has ever permitted the faithful absolute liberty of opinion about its dogmas. Religion and philosophy, for this reason, are incompatible. Of course, Christianity provides a philosophy of personality. But this refers to a limited personality from which the marrow, freedom of thought, about religion has been extracted. This is because reason, without limitations, leads to heresy. There you have the thousand-year battle against free thinking, which is especially characteristic of Kommunists in all epochs. The bodies of John Huss, of Jerónimo of Prague, of Giordano Bruno were devoured by voracious flames because they carried human freedom beyond the frontiers permitted by religious controls. In contrast, Savonarola was burned alive for trying to lift religion out of the low estate to which it had fallen, thanks to the sensual bourgeois conduct of the high ecclesiastics. Ignacio de Loyola was on the point of suffering the same flaming fate because he wanted to subordinate faith to reason. Whereas Voltaire, the most corrosive of all freethinkers, was a friend of Popes, Cardinals, and Archbishops.

Despite the case of Voltaire, the Church fought and keeps on fighting those who consider themselves authorized to build their own spiritual life and select their own road to salvation. Complete autonomy is characteristic of freethinkers. They speak of autonomous science, even of autonomous religion. They believe they can do without God and his Church, which is Catholic. Such men, intrenched in their own spiritual camp, do not wish to be helped by revealed truth and insist on finding it in their own way. The Church despises them and persecutes them. Freethinkers or Kommunists: it's all the same.

Precisely because of this, liberalism (the current doctrine) and freethinkers (as a privileged class) took defensive positions centuries ago. They took advantage of the grotesque spectacle given the world by Emperors and Popes at the beginning of the modern era, and strengthened the State under the Monarchs. Thereby the Catholic Church lost the battle for worldly goods, for political power and influence in temporal affairs. In Italy the new

132

Liberal State corralled the Church at the end of the nine-teenth century, tore away its last feudal possessions, and silenced the Vatican in the world's political affairs.

But of all these losses, one hurt most; that in which political power and spiritual power link hands: the education of children, adolescents, and young people. The Liberal State took as a basic principle the suppression of all dogmatic teaching and the establishment of uniform, obligatory, and free education. Science instead of religion. Religious instruction should be outside the schools of the State. This was known as laicism: the laic school means liberty with regard to dogmas, whatever dogma. The new generations, at least in the primary and secondary grades, should receive an interpretation of historical and scientific facts undistorted by the deformations imposed by religion of any kind. After he is twenty years of age, and the student's knowledge cannot be injured, religion can operate. Thus religious monopoly gave way to state monopoly.

*　　*　　*

In September, 1949, little Guatemala had the pleasure of inviting the Latin American universities to meet together for the first time in history to discuss fundamental problems. As a result of that first Congress, the Union of Latin American Universities was founded, an ancient dream of the Latin people on this continent and one of the serious steps for the defense of endangered values. My government was generous to the Congress and, up until 1953, the Union had received $104,222 from the entire continent, of which Guatemala contributed $76,540. And we gave the new institution a $50,000 headquarters.

133

ANTI-KOMMUNISM IN LATIN AMERICA

All this is brought back to mind by the Colombian sacerdote, Doctor Alfonso Uribe y Misas, Rector of a Catholic University. The titled Rector went to Mexico in May, 1954, to the First Anti-Kommunist Congress meeting there and took as his contribution a pamphlet in which he fulminated against good Guatemala and its suspicious munificence in cultural matters.[8] Referring to the gifts of my government to the Congress and the Union of Universities, the angry sacerdote said: "There are gifts which kill and in this instance the victim is Latin American Catholicism." But his chief fury was vented against the *Recomendaciones y Resoluciones* of the University Congress, a forest of words from which "stick up the ears of the Communist wolf." Therein he said, "one could not read once the word 'Christian,' and this was a symptom of 'religious skepticism,' perhaps even worse, of . . . paganism."

Those recommendations had fallen into such sins as defending the freedom of investigation, of teaching, of academic and scholarly freedom, the free independent school. All this, he believed, had a strong savor of anti-Catholicism: i.e., it was *laic,* ergo *Kommunist.* The Rector descended then from the ideological level, to denounce Russia "and her satellites." He warned that the Mexican Constitution of 1917 implanted Socialist education, and the Constitution of Spain in 1934 prohibited the religious orders from participating in private business and education. Uribe y Misas was not content until he had picked on Guatemala—in the same scandalous manner in those same days of May as the Senators and Congressmen of the United States were doing. "Today there has been launched on our continent a relentless war against Christian doctrine, a war directed from the general headquarters of Guatemala, an

134

American satellite of Soviet Russia." The vehement sacerdote ended by proposing that instead of the Latin American Union of Universities, there be organized a . . . Panamerican University Union, not excluding Puerto Rico, the Hawaiian Islands and . . . Formosa! But the anti-Kommunists of our day do not confine themselves to speech-making. When Guatemala was invaded, a month after the Mexican Congress, the Latin American Union of Universities was expelled from the country. It had to emigrate to Mexico. The reason for its expulsion was its laicism and Latin Americanism, two symptoms of Kommunism. Thus did the new order break into the National Palace of Guatemala with a swish of priestly robes and—it spoke in English.

This battle against laicism has been thundering for some years in Latin America. It is a battle directed by the Catholic Church, while the Empire fights its own battle against other aspects of democracy. In Guatemala laicism and popular government tumbled down together. We cannot speak of a downfall of laicism in Colombia because there, it appears, the Church has never lost political command. The Archbishop of Bogotá has been "to this day" the *Great Elector* of the Republic, said Venezuelan writer Laureano Vallenilla Lanz in 1929.[9] A Laureano it had to be—but a Gómez and a Colombian—who took it upon himself to converse with Franco and to bring to a country of philologists the stink of anti-Kommunism. [This reference is to Conservative Party leader, ex-president Laureano Gómez, who during the World War was the most ardent pro-Hitler and bitter anti-United States figure on the continent. But he changed his tune, at least outwardly, when he was taken under the wing of General George

135

Marshall and the United States at the 1948 Bogotá conference, an attitude which appalled all Latin America, raised a storm among the Colombian people, and contributed to the dreadful *Bogotazo* or destruction of Bogotá. Gómez became President when the ultra-Conservative and Catholic party, with about a third of the electorate, proceeded to slaughter Liberal Party members in tens of thousands by means of the Army and Air Force, even though there was no revolt—one of the worst horrors, though not told to the American people, of our century. —Translator]

Great Argentina has suffered tragically from this war since 1943, when the pro-Hitler clergy and militarists invaded the Casa Rosada, the presidential mansion. The first presidential speech of that "revolution" was prepared by a priest. We in the University representing the Liberal and secular "Old Guard" saw the anti-Kommunist revenge from the inside, which was launched against the sympathizers of Franklin D. Roosevelt. From that day to this, the Argentina debate has been between democracy and its persecutors. What is happening in this respect in Ecuador? What is happening in Costa Rica? In other words, "What is left of laicism in Latin America?" The Catholic Church has backed the laicists—i.e., French liberalism, into a corner, but austere science does not change nor can it be intimidated. "The enemies of laicism are also the enemies of liberty," the popular leader Carlos Sánchez Viamonte has just cried out, in *El Pensemiento Liberal Argentino en el Siglo XIX* (Buenos Aires, 1957, p. 38). The magazine *Sarmiento* directed by Gaspar Mortillaro is also consecrated to the difficult fight, tirelessly and without cowardice. For men of this broad-mindedness there

136

can be no vacillation. An Uribe y Misas y Repiques can confuse the university platform with the pulpit: mix Socialism and Communism, link Guatemala to Russia, join English and Spanish, tie together Colombia with Hawaii, and substitute an Eliécer Gaitán with a Mister Nixon.

[Eliécer Gaitán was the great popular, Liberal Party leader of Colombia who was murdered on the streets of Bogotá during the 1948 Pan American Conference, a deed which precipitated what is called the *Bogotazo,* when the angered populace wrecked and burned down half the city, razing whole skyscrapers and attacking the National Palace. One Pan American delegate hid out under the coffins in a funeral parlor all night.—Translator]

But in Latin America, "thank God," there are still those who denounce such an ideological hodgepodge and ecclesiastical revanchismo, which is not religion; there are still those who cherish and preserve their scholarship and their thought over and beyond the wave of confusion in this turbulent river on which we navigate.

* * *

In child gymnasiums, there is a slide called the toboggan. The toboggan appeals to little ones who laugh as they slide and laugh still more when they fall on the mattress of sand. For adults, on the other hand, the toboggan is dangerous, an even greater danger for those who dedicate themselves to the slippery sport of persecuting the crime of ideas. To throw oneself down this slope provides a pleasing dizziness, which momentarily befogs the "faculties" as in the beginning of a fainting spell.

137

This happens in the police suppression of ideas, of dangerous ideas, which at first are "deviations," then are sins. This occurred with a Chilean sacerdote of crystal-clear professional rectitude, Monseñor José María Caro, Bishop of Iquique in 1918 and now (1958) Prime Cardinal of Chile. In no way does he resemble that Archbishop of Guatemala whom we saw helping the United Fruit to recover what that commercial enterprise considered belonged to it. José María Caro, born and raised in a patriotic climate, the climate of which Chileans are so proud, at the end of the century made his apostolate a clean page of life. His ninety years find him, as at fifty, in Iquique, serving Chile, the Chileans, and the Catholic Church. Never have the English-speaking enterprises that chew up Chilean copper and nitrate found in him a hypocritical accomplice or a corrupt servitor. Of such examples are the better legion of Catholic priests, and it is because of them that the Church, fighting in so many storms during the nineteenth century, has been able to survive and be reborn so powerfully in the middle of the twentieth.

But even from the hand of this impeccable spokesman for Christ, we also slip down the toboggan. Already we have been told that laicism is tainted with Kommunism. Monseñor Caro helps us further down the slide, by taking us back through history to discover that *Masonry is Kommunism.* Dispersed secret societies founded around 1400 in Central Europe were federated under the English sky in 1717. From there they returned full blown to the continent and crossed the Atlantic toward Boston, following the route of the *Mayflower.* A religious sect, an international brotherhood, a revolutionary organization—positive not anarchistic—Masonry, which had as members the highest personages in each country, including State functionaries, even Monarchs, soon came into conflict with the Catholic Church. Protected by Christian symbols such as the Bible and the Cross, hidden behind enigmatic rites, fallen into practices a bit infantile, Masonry was pledged to provide an esoteric science and some day deliver an as yet nonexistent secret philosophy. In armed struggle against fanaticism and intolerance, Masonry succeeded in strengthening its resources and in systematically displacing representatives of the Vatican. Making use of the astuteness and wariness which persist as vestiges in that contradictory entity known as the human being, Masonry planned battles in the shadows and launched tempests in the light of day. Or at least participated in an important way in those battles.

Secret societies were forbidden from the middle of the eighteenth century by Popes Clement XI and Benedict XIV, and again received *pontifical censure* by Pius VII in 1821 and by Leo XII in 1825. According to Pope Pius VII in 1830, such societies caused "great damage to religion and the Empires." A specific condemnation of Masonry did not occur until Gregory XV (1831-46). The fact was, religion and the Empires had nothing pleasant to expect from this powerful fraternity which grew mysteriously until it established itself in every corner of the globe. But it was Leo XIII in the 1884 *Humanum Genus Encyclical,* who gave the clear-cut cry of alarm, declaring from Saint Peter's See that throughout the world *Masonry* and *Communism* and *Socialism* signified the same thing.

Monseñor José María Caro published a book in 1918 corroborating this.[10] He said, concerning a "Universal Conspiracy" against the altar, the throne, and private property

(p. 226), "Masonry has as its final end socialism," including the nationalization of big enterprises (p. 227). It is a conspiracy against society, against religion, the Fatherland and the family (p. 40), to the point of destroying all authority (p. 47). According to Monseñor Caro, Masonry has as its supreme aspiration the return of man to his natural state (p. 45). Once he is in this natural state, Masonry will put forth a new religion: the worship of Lucifer (pp. 106, 126, 133, 147). This worship will cause the Masons to combat not only Christianity but all atheism, a posture that can be reconciled, according to the Catholic author, by means of Emancipated Reason (p. 150). For a long time Masonry used one mask: the Liberal Party. Now it serves radicalism, socialism, and Communism (p. 162).

But Monseñor is unable to stop in his downward slide in linking up so many evils together. He goes so far as to tell us that Masonry is also tied up with Judaism, with Paganism, with Theosophy, and Magic (pp. 128-31, 282-87). "All or nearly all the authors I have been able to see," he states on page 226, "established the doctrinal kinship between Masonry and the systems destructive of social order," and "the authors of our days make it clear that Judaism is intimately related to Masonry and to revolutionary parties, from Socialism to Bolshevism." But its goal would not be the dictatorship of the proletariat, but the destruction of Christianity (p. 226) in order to establish Jewish predominance in the world (p. 49). Henry Ford in Chapter XIX of Part I of *El Judío Internacional* (The International Jews) reaches the same conclusions as Monseñor Caro.

The evil of all this down-the-toboggan argumentation

140

THE CATHOLIC CHURCH AND ITS ANTI-KOMMUNISM

is that Monseñor Caro, in confirming that the existence of an alliance between religion and the empires, of which Pope Pius VIII spoke, enumerates and describes as Masonic, that is to say Kommunist, the greatest human achievements in the way of democratic progress. Work of the Masons and Kommunists have been:

The English revolution which sent Charles I to the gibbet in 1649.

The expulsion of the Jesuits from Portugal (1759) and Spain (1767).

The emancipation of the Thirteen English Colonies in America (1776).

The French Revolution of 1789 ("the cursed conspiracy!")

The emancipation of the Spanish colonies in America, from 1810 to 1824.

The Second French Revolution, of 1848.

The Mexican insurrection against Emperor Maximilian, shot in 1867.

The political and social reform brought about in Mexico and in Guatemala from 1860 to 1875.

Italian unification (1859-70).

The installation of the Spanish Republic in 1931.

As can be seen, the confluence of documents or pseudo-documents has led Monseñor Caro to associate Masonry and Communism with all those revolutionary popular and national events, which left as their outcome the downfall of various monarchies, the weakening of a number of empires and the implantation of democratic systems in Europe and America. By his implacable crusade against

Masonry, Monseñor Caro's book endows Masonry and Communism with credit for the greatest glories of modern and contemporary history. Even more: Masons and Communists, according to him, have been the leaders of these movements, and included many of the most eminent political leaders and writers, which the intellectuals of our time still venerate: Cromwell, Washington, Danton, Robespierre, Bonaparte, Bolívar, Andrés Bello, San Martín, Sucre, Garibaldi, Mazzini, Martí, Maceo, Proudhon, Goethe, Herder, Heine, Lessing, Carducci, Victor Hugo, Lord Byron, Lincoln, Benito Juárez, Sarmiento, Emerson, Rodó, González Prada, Juan Montalvo, Batlle y Ordóñez, D'Annunzio, Yrigoyen, Alessandri, Plutarco Elías Calles, César Augusto Sandino. . . . Masons and . . . Kommunists would be, according to Monseñor Caro's slippery argumentation: the Ku Klux Klan, the institution of Boy Scouts, the Arbor Day festival of the tree (pure paganism), the pedagogical movement which advocates the "escuela única" (the single school), the Y.M.C.A., the League for the Defense of Human Rights, the International Association of Universities, etc.

There is no doubt that Masonry of all epochs and in every country has vigorously attacked clericalism, that is to say the intervention of the clergy in local politics. For the same reason, it has directed its fire against the papacy in an effort to diminish its tremendous hegemony over European kings and emperors and over the petty presidents and mighty police power in Latin America. And we shall not mention the United States, where Masonry went forth from its temples to the skyscrapers and the banks, and from them to the Pentagon. "American gold," as Monseñor confesses on page 153, was active in more than a few of these Masonic and Kommunist "cataclysms," and Puerto Rico, he says, is a booty won Masonic-style by the heretics of the Potomac. What do you say about that, Monseñor Rossell y Arellano?

But, whether it be true or false that the Masons have sworn war to the death on clericalism, there is no justification, whatever the hatred of the combatants, that obliges us to admit, as Monseñor Caro desires, that *democracy* is the legitimate daughter of Masonry (year 1400) and its belated concubine, Marxist Communism (1850). It does not soothe us or upset us that Pius VIII insisted that Masonry is a danger for the Empires. We know, to be sure, that the papacy maintained and maintains a brotherly alliance with the Empires. We understand the fears over the collapse of thrones and the roll of crowned heads. No small number of sacerdotes and Bishops lived their juicy lives with Princesses and Princes, with Monarchs and Emperors and, along with them, at the same time, lost their lives. The blood of priests was spilled, together with that of the nobles and feudal lords, at the foot of the guillotine. At the same time there were sacerdotes who rose up in the name of Christ against the ruthless feudal system. A great and glorious Republic of the Americas (México) was born from the fiery sermons and lofty heroism of two Catholic sacerdotes. Years afterwards, this same nation would commit the horrible Masonic and Kommunist crime of shooting a foreign Prince, imported into Mexico to be Emperor. The pages of Monseñor Caro's own book, which degenerates from a chute into a labyrinth, inform us that the *Bonaparte family* operated under Masonic (Kommunist) orders.

The sending of Maximilian on a French mission to

143

Mexico, would therefore be a Masonic transatlantic message. But pages before that we were informed that his execution was also the doings of Masonry. As a result of watching so many heads of Princes and sacerdotes roll in the dust, we no longer faint away when the poor head of common sense also rolls on the ground dry and bloodless, without the beating of drums. Benito Juárez—Kommunist! Maximilian, also! Monseñor Caro, a Mason too?

(Without any doubt, Masonry and Communism are antagonistic doctrines. In any event this is the official thinking of Masonry. *O'Malhete,* Masonic publication of Saõ Paulo, sets this out clearly in its heading. And a Canadian sacerdote, of whom we shall speak presently, affirms that the Communist governments closed Masonic lodges.)[11]

The secret of this mésalliance of concepts in this tumultuous river for invisible fishers, resides in the fact that Masonry and Liberalism were associated as leaders and theoreticians, during the political and social conquest by the European and American peoples in the nineteenth century. It would be very difficult to disassociate these conquests of the popular emancipation movement from the word democracy. That the Catholic Church had been closely in league with the old powers of absolutism was not the fault of the peoples who struggled for their freedom, winning by tooth and nail a little more space in which to live, to breathe, to grow a bit within the enormous imperial and ecclesiastical possessions.

During the hard fight, the Empires and the Church suffered the same fate. While one lost crowns and heads, noble titles, feudal domain, and great estates, the other lost its own plantations, farms, vineyards, and orchards and, along with its many castles and enormous treasures, lost

144

also its political privileges, its earthly command, its civic and social leadership. The separation of Church and State, the suppression of monasteries and convents, the expropriation of ecclesiastical properties, the installation of the civil registry to replace the old parish book, the laws of civil matrimony and divorce, the prohibition of the practicing of religious rites in the street, the establishment of compulsory free secular schooling, were the chief chapters in the political defeat of the Church, up until that time all-powerful. The Yankee Masons even came to speak of the "tyranny of Rome" over men, referring to its old ties and secret influence over all aspects of terrestrial life. And Liberalism, in the whole world, especially French liberalism, did not conceal its plans for democratic revindication in an open fight against clericalism.

It is not surprising, therefore, that in this hour of anti-Kommunist hysteria, the Catholic Church attempts to recover what it lost and denounces as a Kommunist adventure, the adventure in behalf of democracy. In order to restore the waters to turn its mill, it does not shirk from the herculean task of exhuming the glories of the Empires, the sanctity of monarchical rights, and the handing over of the crowns of another day to the new Caesars of Catholicism: Mussolini, Franco, Laureano Gómez, Trujillo. Is this not the sure way to recover the enormous properties that have been lost? Yes, this is surely the way. But this is not and never was the way of Christ.

* * *

If we turn our eyes from the land of Chile to the country of Uribe y Misas, we shall find the entrance to another cave where we can come upon another trail of anti-

Kommunism. At our first uncertain steps on this road, we shall give our hand to one of America's greatest, General-issimo of Land, Sea, and Air, President of the Republic, Gustavo Rojas Pinilla. This much praised Police-State ruler of recent vintage is unable to conceal his love for the Holy Mother Catholic Church and places in its powerful custody the lives of the Colombians and the gold of the Treasury of the Republic. To a sensitive soul such as his, agonized by mysticism—as is also that of his compatriot and colleague, Laureano Gómez—the Catholic religion should be imposed as the universal religion, with this difference: that Rojas Pinilla would begin with Pan American religious rule under the directives of the Organization of American States.

With such aims, in August, 1953 (according to the credible information of the United Press), this spiritual mentor of the Colombians—the same one who months later ordered the terrifying police brutality in the bull-ring—this foremost Catholic of the country, with a mahogany prayer bench and a vermilion cushion for the eleven o'clock mass, with a seat reserved in heaven, attacked non-Catholic services, stating that the activity of Protestant missionaries in Colombia constituted "the greatest danger for national unity and American solidarity." This Protestant activity, he added, was the reason Colombians were losing their religious faith and "lent themselves to international creeds." We are struck by this expression, "international creeds." The Police Ruler is certain, apparently, that Jesus Christ was born in Bucaramanga.

This academic reference to international creeds puts us on the right road. The presidential voice has stated it.

Three years later in February, 1956, the Bishop of Ibagué, known as Arturo Duque Villegas, ordered the excommunication of fathers and teachers who sent their sons or pupils to the educational centers founded or run by Protestants. The problem of excommunication is a serious matter. But though the popes excommunicated and slit each other's throats in the golden age of the Vatican, and if that is why so many Princes and Emperors were excommunicated and beheaded, we do not get goosepimples on learning that the Colombian plebes will be excommunicated en masse by a decree from a mere Creole. The grave aspect of the matter is that this thirst for Paradise is not restricted to Palace oratory or threats from the pulpit. In the period of eight years up to 1957, *forty-seven Protestant churches and chapels were burned down or dynamited* in Colombia. *Seventy-six Protestants were killed.* Their crime: having worshipped Christ in their own way. The accusation was leveled by the Council of Churches of Florida in April, 1957, according to *El Mercurio*, April 26, 1957. In such matters, the Colombians of this epoch of the "free world" have invented nothing new. The modern history of Europe was written with the blood of believers, and the burning torch raced across continents and oceans, passing from hand to hand, as in the Olympic Games. Religious faith, when it sinks to fanaticism, is capable of any and everything; even more so if the commands are issued by people forgotten by God.

But superior voices keep the flame alive, or cleverly provide the burning pitch, or indicate what tree will make the best torch, or how to transport it most rapidly. His Holiness Pope Pius XII, for example, on inaugurating the

Apostolic Secular Congress (like the word nationalism, "secular" is sometimes a useful word), in October, 1957, pointed out that among the dangers in Latin America for the Catholic Church were *Protestantism and Communism* (*El Mercurio*, October 6, 1957). When, years before, Rojas Pinilla ridiculed international creeds, it seemed to suggest (with police-style maliciousness) that Protestantism and Communism walked side by side. Now the Holy Pope no longer suggested it; he stated it. He stated it as a message for exportation to Latin America. Because in Latin America, Protestantism is not convenient. Fruitful, in contrast, it has been for the North American people "whose charity towards those who suffer and whom they see oppressed in all parts of the world, is truly worthy of the best Christian traditions." [12] But this charity is Protestant, because it has been the official charity of a nation that was long ruled only by Protestants. And *His Holiness* could not have denied either that he himself took *the side of Russia* with the "fullest collaboration" in those tragic days, when, in the words of his High Pontifice, love, law, and justice fought against hate, force, and selfishness. [13] On the side of love, law, and justice stood Russia. In that hour of universal tribulation, Protestantism, Communism, Catholicism were love, law, and justice.

But in 1957, His Holiness, the Pope, said not so. Above all not for Latin America. Thus we do not become alarmed when in the magazine *Estudios Sobre el Comunismo* (April-June, 1954) of Santiago de Chile, an unsuspected Hispanist named Sergio Mirofanda Carrington, tells us in an article entitled "Hispanidad y Comunismo," "Responsible North American circles, who encourage and perhaps finance the so-called *'Protestant pastors'* who are arriving by thousands on these shores, thereby aid Communism. These peoples will remain Catholics or after a brief sojourn with Protestantism will fall into atheism. *From Protestantism to Communism* is for us only a short step." "After a brief time with Protestantism": it gives us chills, the idea this gentleman has of time. Three hundred and fifty years of Protestantism has not converted the United States into a Communist country. Just the opposite. Protestantism has been the chief driving force of its financial growth and its phobia against Communism. Mirofanda and Rojas Pinilla do not know that. But this misconception of time is not the most striking thing; we are more shocked by the space concept of the Hispanist. "From Protestantism to Communism is only a brief step." We shall examine what has happened and find out just how short or long the step really is.

* * *

In the first place, that which eventually was called *Protestantism* originated as a movement within *Catholicism*, a movement which sought to cure the universal prostration of the Roman Church by evangelical medicines. It came midst scarcely edifying quarrels between the Pontifices and aspirants for succession. It came when "indulgences" were used to exploit believers, when clerics were corrupt and viciously sensual. When all this threatened to put an end to the authority of Catholicism, and the dangers of a moral drought, even the disappearance of the Church, were visible to all, there arose the "protest" of the mystics and the experimental discipline of new ascetics, and the

149

crushing logic of other theologies as a dissidence—fresh branching out from the same grandiose tree. It was a family rebellion to reform the Roman ecclesiastical system. Without this tremendous shaking up, without such an upheaval, Christianity would have sunk out of sight. Instead, Rome could have talked about a Catholicism no longer medieval but modern, thanks to the new Catholic sect, which kept on preaching Reform. But defending its system, the Roman Church, rigid and intolerant, obliged the dissidents to establish a separate church, which within a few years in turn would display equal intolerance and rigidity.

Very well. This anguish, this desperate protest, which strives to pass from the superficial (ecclesiastic) to the interior (Biblical) truth; which wishes to return to the direct word of God and join with it even in the shadows, almost pantheistically, without the intermediation of terrestrial "authorities" so completely discredited (a Borgian Pope burned a Savonarola); this mystical thirst for the divine and the eternal in all its purity; this universal rebirth of faith and compassion; this search of the Holy Scriptures as the one body of religion, with consequent disdain for ecclesiastical "tradition"—all this, nothing more than Catholic fervor and Catholic discontent, was going to convert itself (who would ever have imagined it!) into Kommunism.

If the Christian decides to save himself by doing good works and by more devoted service to God, by disregarding the confessor and sacerdotes considered illegitimate, it is because he is an individual stained with the sin of pride, and hence . . . a Kommunist. If the religious be-

liever is inspired by his own faith to the point of despera-
tion and seeks God intimately, beyond what the old theology deemed proper, he is a revolutionary, therefore a
Kommunist. If the Christian revaluates man and speaks of
the man's "honor"—even the "saintliness of man"—and
gives new credit to his potentialities so that he ceases to be
mere floss that can be blown away by the slightest celestial
puff, thereby he limits God's liberty, becomes a pedant,
hence a Kommunist.

Without the slightest doubt, Catholics and pseudo-
Catholics who hold this opinion grant to Communism
(that is to say, Marxist materialism) a spiritual content
which it lacks: i.e., esteem for the high value of man as an
individual. Perhaps this is because any such human excel-
lence, as preached by the Protestant dissidents, and man's
possible grandeur as a man can be gained only by an in-
ferred theft of the infinite treasures of an infinite God.
It can be obtained only by looting that ocean of perfection, with the danger that it may be exhausted. And this
"robbery" of the goods of others, even in the spiritual
domain, is Kommunism. It is an expropriation by force!

Already in the classic era, paganism came to declare
that illustrious men were like gods. Protestantism and
paganism walked hand and hand into heresy. And since
Monseñor Caro demonstrated that Communism and
paganism are synonymous (thanks to Masonry and Judaism), then Protestantism and Kommunism are also
identical.

We shall find the beginning of an explanation if we
recall that this modernist movement of innovation within
Catholicism—in some things orthodox, in others heterodox

151

—had advanced a little further to the point of insisting on a transformation of the structure of that Church, a reform in the clerical manner it was being administered. Later they would speak of the suppression of images as objects of worship, of a new style in the mass, of a different form of prayer, of a sterner morality, to the point of remaking the doctrine itself and its dogmatism. And in the next breath, they would propose a selection among the sacerdotes (mostly sinners) and the return to ancient institutions, to the purity of earlier conduct—in a word, to an exemplary life. A cataclysm seemed to threaten to shake the foundations of Rome. (And the cataclysm struck, not from the hullabaloo of the Protestants, but from the invasion of the apostolic city by the troops of the most powerful Catholic emperor of the epoch, Charles V, and the sacking of the Holy City in 1527.) There is the wherefore of the stubborn defensive position of Roman Catholicism. If to this it is added that Protestantism was born of and fed by a certain Teutonic nationalism (which Rojas Pinilla was ignorant of even in 1953), which desired to break with what they called Caesarian Popery and with Imperial Rome, as well as with the ancient theology, even to the extent of establishing a "Church of Saints," or professing faithful or saintly livers—with occasional references to "primitive Communism"—we have another explanation for the Roman defense of what was Roman.

True enough, Protestant tolerance, which permitted the faithful to start a plurality of churches and subjects, did not lack the democratic spirit. Furthermore the birth of Protestantism gave the opportunity and the pretext for armed popular uprisings against authority and later on produced a theory of the right of resistance and insurrection against injustice even to the point of justifying tyrannicide. Mixed in with all this, according to Troeltsch, was a certain "mystic, spiritual dissolvent of Churches," born and augmented in the heat of the Reform. Protestant sects came to curse the laws and traditions which crushed the free development of individual conscience. Also the Protestants, like the Masons, associated the Bible with the sword, and more than once Protestant books have been designated as the organ of the Masonic sect of the Rosicrucians. And a Protestant pastor introduced Masonry into France! It is also true that a Protestant sect came to merit the designation of "evangelical Communism," the sect of the Moravian Brotherhood.

Similarly, it cannot be denied, the breakdown of the formidable ecclesiastical unity of Roman Catholicism opened the doors to something like religious anarchy, which gave each intelligence the right to choose its own road to the experiencing of God. And true it is, finally, that Karl Marx and Protestantism clasped hands in the high cathedral of Hegel. This is why Troeltsch says: "The Catholic critique is accustomed to see in Protestantism the revolutionary spirit of the modern world."[14]

Good enough; this "revolutionary spirit" is what has produced the existing democratic organization of Europe and America. To "blame" Protestantism for that is to confess at once that one is anti-democratic. To call the Protestant religious movement and Masonry *Kommunist* for having contributed to the achieving of an anti-monarchical, anti-totalitarian institutional life, is to confess oneself a partisan of monarchy and dictatorship. And

153

this is the major mistake of the contemporary Falangist clergy and their allies such as the mystical Rojas Pinilla and the Hispanophile Mirofanda. [Falangist refers to a follower of "Christian Fascism" as developed under Franco of Spain and diffused throughout Latin America.—Translator]

From this point of view, we must realize that Protestantism does not predicate the subordination of the State to the Church, but rather that State and Church should live on an equal level, having as their single superior "authority" the Biblical texts. Its nationalism is far indeed from totalitarian universality. In Protestantism there is, in fact, a certain "sympathy" for democracy. Contemporary sociologists relate Calvin's doctrine to the origin of modern capitalism.[15] Protestants, without any doubt, were the navigators of the *Mayflower*, and they were to "blame"— especially the Puritans and Baptists—for establishing the religious-civic foundations of democracy in America, thus going against the monarchical principles of the Roman Church and the authoritarianism of the Anglican Church. From this side of the Atlantic, they mocked at both totalitarian systems: The United States of North America, exclusively the product of Protestantism, is considered by journalists "as the first democracy in the world." The cruel irony is that that country and its present rulers, which are at this time anti-Communist, are running neck and neck with the Catholic Church, though pursuing different ends.

Things, however, have not come to flower in such a simplified way. Luther felt a repugnance he could not hide for the illiterate masses and came to theorize adversely on the democratic spirit being born in Europe. It

154

is no secret that Luther, a Conservative, came to define himself as an Absolutist and conducted himself as a partisan of a certain Prussianism. At times Zwingli also often acted like a dictator. Calvin, for his part, because of the exigencies of the struggle, came to establish a State Church in a State both religious and police-ruled, thus providing the methods which in our day most please the gendarmes.

On various occasions, Protestantism by the imperatives of obtaining order and authority—they, too!—set up new hierarchies, other kinds of Popes and new kinds of Caesars, with the same tyrannical features and the very same armed troops "to persuade" recalcitrant Catholics. They came to accuse them of theocratic dictatorship and polygamy. And on occasions, they had to make use of that vengeful "barbaric justice" of which Catholicism was accused. They, too, came to outlaw, sentence and . . . murder nonbelievers and heretics. Finally the demon of flesh, for centuries catastrophic for the Catholic clergy, did not fail to visit the Protestant pastors in the intimate precincts of their cloisters.

It is very confusing to know that, even so, the nobility, the "enlightened Princes" and the feudal landlords (still feudal), embraced Protestantism from its very beginning. And even more, that the ultra-Catholic Carlos V came to legalize Lutheranism in Germany. For one advantage favored Protestantism: it strengthened the ties between State and Church without subordinating either. This is its maximum sin in the eyes of Rome: that of maintaining the State and Church on equal levels. What Rome forgets is that Protestantism succeeded in keeping the State within an official religious climate. In contrast, in the *eyes of*

Moscow the sin of Protestantism is that of continuing to be a religion based on spiritual dogmas. This interesting aspect was revealed in August, 1948, when the Ecumenical Assembly of Christianity was celebrated in Amsterdam; both Rome and Moscow denied permission to attend to the sacerdotes they controlled. It seemed the reunion was tainted with "Protestantism." Neither the Catholics nor the Communists were there!

* * *

Even so, in this front line of combat against Kommunism, spokesmen for the clergy are accustomed to embellish their propaganda with a shameful confession of democratic faith and attack the adversary by calling him a "danger" for Western democracy, or they simplify things even more by attacking him as an enemy of the powerful ally of Catholicism, the United States. Conservatism, liberalism, secularism, Masonry, Protestantism are left in an obscure, fetid pig-sty, with a tag on their chests: Kommunists. That is to say, for the clericals we have mentioned: enemies of the Catholic faith and enemies of democracy.

Such ambivalence has been denounced and proscribed by a Canadian Catholic sacerdote and university professor born in Hungary, Aurèle Kolnai,[16] in his *Errors of Anti-Communism.*

In his opinion (p. 15) this simulation of loyalty to democracy, Western or not, is most prejudicial. Communism should be fought without allies and without false masks: and especially if in the end these allies should turn out to be, as he proceeds to prove, contaminated with . . . Kommunism. *Loyalty to the Church and nothing else!* insists

Kolnai. Then: how clear the heavens, the landscape, and the road! The United States is thus taken out of the anti-Kommunist set-up. Was it an accident that the *cynic* (p. 86), the *imbecile* (p. 95) , Franklin Delano Roosevelt, aided the Communist victory in Europe? Kolnai refers to certain North American circles, calling them "bourgeois brains with fatty degeneration" (p. 112). A little further on (p. 131): "the bourgeoisie, breathing idealism and insulting Communism, are a spectacle too ridiculous to provoke even satire."

For Kolnai the Catholic Church should remain alone because it is sufficient unto itself. This solitary role in the struggle produces cleanliness, energy, efficacy. Now, at last, we know what ground we are treading and where we are going.

For Kolnai, Communism is anti-Christ, to the extent that it is a parody of Christ (pp. 128-29) , a parody complicated with a "unique and unprecedented hatred" of Christ. Communism is the enemy of Christ, of the Church and its believers. More than a political doctrine or a system of social organization, Communism is religion: a universal religion that audaciously seeks to substitute the Catholic religion (p. 79) with the satanic promise of a terrestrial Paradise, and which appropriates for its own advantage the promises of the Evangel (p. 128).

But it is an execrable religion "because essentially it is defiance of the sovereignty of God" (p. 63). It is religion without God. *"Obligatory atheism,"* he calls it further on p. 118; "essential and integral atheism" (p. 126) . Better said: a God different from the God of Judaic-Christian tradition. This transcendent God, prior to man, creator of

157

man and man's shape, does not exist for Marxist materialists. Communism admits of no God except man himself—not man as an individual, but man in the mass, as a collectivity of the human species. Communism does not even permit a plurality of deities as paganism does. Obviously the religious essence of this fanatic and salvationist policy is to attempt to establish its power in the world as total and unique (p. 23).

Scientific socialism is for them like a natural law universally imposed (p. 27). But it is better described as *"Satanism"* that seeks to possess the entire man in order to carry him on to "cosmic subversion" (p. 33). On the other hand, Kolnai reminds us that Catholicism is not one of a number of faiths possible for human conscience; it is the only religion, the only faith, which every human being, to the degree he is a human being, should profess (p. 122). And so we come to understand that the counterpositions of Catholicism and Communism are something inevitable, something irreconcilable; between them lies an abyss that cannot be bridged (p. 148). There, too, is the source of the *war unto death* between two religious worlds.

Face up to it: Communism is a formidable foe. One of the many errors of anti-Kommunism, according to Kolnai, is in believing Communism to be fragile or weak. With this enemy, there can be no transaction, no truce, no appeasement (p. 117). This terrible adversary must be met by an all-out fight without resort to mutilated or petty truths (pp. 15, 45). Neither is Kolnai interested in the arguments of the "anti-Moscow progressives," from orthodox liberals to Trotskyites and Titoists, or other resentful leftists, embittered and disillusioned, mouthing reproaches at Communism for not having been loyal to Marxian doctrine (p. 48). He is not interested because the enemy is not merely what is superficially understood to be Communism.

To combat Communism we must *also combat its antecedents and its causes.* Antecedents of Communism are: bourgeois democracy (p. 23) and industrial civilization (p. 89). Bourgeois democracy as well as Communism are caught in the same swamp of prejudices and economic values. A certain "vulgar Marxism" has penetrated capitalism, which in the Western world is a "disguised totalitarianism" (p. 159). The bourgeois democrat, like the Communist, depends on economic advantages. He is like a passive slave of Marxism (p. 23).

In short, for Kolnai, there is an "historic continuity" among all Left movements (orthodox liberalism, social democracy, Socialism) and the Bolshevik regime (p. 51). Communism is nothing more than the final unfolding of the *theme whispered* by them, "their most enduring characteristic essence and aim," the ultimate achievement of all of them. What are those themes, those hidden aims that actuate the successive stages of this grandiose rush toward Kommunism? Here they are (pp. 51-52):

> Centralization of the State.
> The destruction of all authority and community life not dependent on the State.
> Laicism and Secularization.
> The philosophic conception of an omnipotent "collective will" (Rousseau's "general will") (p. 99).
> The negation of natural law.

159

The negation of hereditary principles and rights.

The conception of government as the embodiment of unitarian social conscience.

The suppression of social inequalities and as a substitute the implantation of a hierarchy of office-holders.

The subjection of all social order to the administrative regime which presumes to represent "the general will."

The materialistic conception that human happiness is in the functioning of technology and physical sciences.

The totalitarian tendency implicit in the effort to interpret everything as a function of the "collective will."

Such sins are perpetrated not merely by the democrats, Socialists, social idealists, revolutionists, and progressives in general, but also even by some right and left Christians who like to talk about "social justice" (pp. 52, 62).

"Today social injustices exist . . . " wrote Pope Pius XII in his letter to Truman, already cited. He called therefore for social justice. Even the pontifical robe, made of the wool of immaculate lambs, is stained with . . . Kommunism.

But the "supreme, ultimate, and absolute characteristic which distinguishes the Communist regime" is its monomaniacal obsession for a "social progress" (p. 53). And this same recurring central theme is at the same time proof of the tie-up with other trends prior to Communism and its blood brothers.

160

A retrospective concept of Communism leads Kolnai to pin down historical and ideological signposts which mark, as some would say, the march of Attila. One of these markers is the French revolution, politically catalogued in the Vatican archives as pre-Socialist. There was, says Kolnai, a "certain anticipation of Communism during the height of the Terror" (p. 59). Another culminating "moment" along Attila's march, is Industrialization, "which was unleashed and also inspired by the liberal doctrine of Adam Smith" (p. 67). The essence of this stage is "political equality" with its resultant "economic equality," and its definite triumph; "universal state regimentation." In this can be seen the "dialectic phases" of this march toward the new god of Progress (p. 67).

On this lofty ground Kolnai pauses briefly to tweak the ear of *the United States*: these "poor North Americans, naive peasants with a shopworn formula of progress." Of the *Utopia of Progress!* (p. 125). Perhaps Utopia for, according to Kolnai, the conditions of man's terrestrial life are unchangeable (p. 106). Also, "Western civilization in its present phase—its society highly industrialized under the regime of liberal democracy—is also atheist and materialistic; it tends to substitute for moral law and a spiritual feeling the life of Progress and Prosperity" (p. 134). In this sense, Communism and Western civilization turn out to be rivals in seeking material goods: they are brothers who dispute over the same gold-and-silver robe. They are, therefore, equally execrable! But Western civilization is not merely characterized by its material goods; besides prosperity, technology, and progress, there is a fourth brutalizing [sic] element, universal education! . . . (p. 152).

161

It is really impossible to discuss Kolnai's series of stupefying generalities. We prefer, therefore, to refrain from commenting on this so-called human brutalization by the diffusion of culture.

They, the North Americans, "sympathetic pedants," believe that "only capitalism is democracy" (p. 69); for they understand democracy as a function of merchandise, prices, and consumers; on the other hand, their "barbaric idol of quantitative prosperity," their "mechanistic, concentrated and materialistic furor" demands that they be governed, to a certain degree, socialistically (pp. 87-88). Ergo, this "industrial civilization"—"and in general modern civilization"—give their hand to Cartesian rationalism in an "essential atheism" beyond redemption, the culmination of which is Communism (p. 89). But still more: this modernism or liberalism or industrialism or equalitarianism "has set up as God, the Needs of Man" (p. 78). The Needs and Rights of Man! But these needs are insatiable and destructive of every moral orientation. And these needs are those they promise to satisfy in a new terrestrial paradise (p. 79).

Equality and Progress, it is clearly seen, are the two poisons that Kommunism has produced. "The Progressive impulse can complete its process only with absolute barbarism, in total nothing" (p. 68). Utopia and the progressive impulse "lead fatally, by their intrinsic nature, to totalitarian barbarism" (p. 72).

Once having tossed aside the democratic mask, Kolnai seizes the sword and launches himself at the other prejudices and poisons and microbes of the Kommunist sickness: "modern thought," Cartesian philosophy, and the pantheistic systems (p. 68). But if there is one thing of which Descartes cannot be accused, it is affinity for Communism. A courtesan in private life, an adulator of princes and princesses, he had to define his anti-democratic and absolutist position to the point of affirming "the divine right of the strong," which did not fall far short of ecclesiastical doctrine. Even more: Descartes' opportunism led him to assume the role of friendly mediator in conflicts between religion and the State. "The Cartesian doubt," a philosophical method which suggests that all dogmas be placed in alcohol, is perhaps what led him to join Pius XII, the predictor of "social justice" in this new corral of Kommunists. (See Leopold Garcés Castiella, *Las Ideas Políticas de Descartes*, Vol. III of *Homenaje a Descartes*, Department of Philosophy and Letters. Buenos Aires, 1937.)

Rationalism and individualism are, in a sense, blood brothers. That is why, for Kolnai, individualism is the tap root of Communism. It is individualism which, destroying all ties of social authority, "has opened the road to the omnipotence of the State" (p. 136). Communism is nothing more than the heir of individualism, its fulfillment, but at the same time its assassin. Yet all this individualistic virus does not originate with Descartes. This individualism which preaches that "man is the measure of all things," was proclaimed by a Greek philosopher, twenty centuries before Descartes. Kommunists the Greeks, too?

This would seem to be too much. But no. For Kolnai it is not sufficient to have carried back the origins of Kommunism to the fifth century before Christ. Kolnai confesses (pp. 137-38) that it is absolutely necessary to go back even further, "much further," to the very origins, when Mal—Evil—was first written with a capital letter. And *this beginning was in Lucifer,* the angel of darkness. Long ago an observer of his time said, "The devil was the first Leftist" (p. 139).

Respectable public: the comedy is over. Too bad that we have ended up in Hell.

NOTES TO CHAPTER IV

1. Joseph Bernhard, *El Vaticano, Potencia Mundial* (The Vatican: World Power) (Barcelona, 1947). The original was in German, and the translation was published "with the proper permission" under Franco's regime.

2. *Ibid.,* pp. 28-29.

3. Osegueda, p. 144.

4. *La Voz Guadalupana* (México) August, 1954, p. 23.

5. Pastoral letter of the Archbishop of Guatemala. In *Estudios sobre el Comunismo* (Santiago de Chile), No. 5, July-September, 1954, pp. 110-13.

6. Michael Schmaus, *Sobre la Esencia del Cristianismo* (On the Essence of Christianity) (Madrid, 1952), p. 224.

7. Bernhard, p. 159.

8. Alfonso Uribe y Misas, *Contra la Intervención Soviética en la América Latina* (Against Soviet Intervention in Latin America) (Medellín), April, 1954.

9. Vallenilla Lanz, p. 322.

10. Jose Maria Caro, *El Misterio de la Masonería* (The Enigma of Freemasonry) (2d edition, Buenos Aires, 1954), 340 pp.

11. Auréle Kolnai, *Errores del Anticomunismo* (Errors of Anti-Communism) (Madrid, 1952), p. 42.

12. Letter from his Holiness to President Truman, August 26, 1947.

13. *Pío XII y Roosevelt. Su Correspondencia durante la Guerra* (Pius XII and Roosevelt. Their Correspondence during the War) (Madrid, 1948), p. 88.

14. Ernst Troeltsch, *El Protestantismo y el Mundo Moderno* (Protestantism and the Modern World) (México, 1951), p. 34. This basic study and that of Emile G. Leonard, *Histoire du Protestantisme* (Paris, 1950), p. 66, can amplify whatever point may be obscure in what we are treating.

15. Gurvitch, p. 126; Leonard, p. 66.

16. We pay homage to the Guatemalan philologist, engineer Lisandro Sandoval, who proposed that the adjective *"canadiense"* [Canadian] be outlawed as incorrect. *Semántica Guatemalteca* (Guatemala, 1941), Vol. 1, pp. 156-57. [In his Spanish text Arévalo uses the form *"canadense,"* proposed by Sandoval, instead of the accepted *"canadiense."*—Translator]

V.

THE GEESE
OF THE
CAPITOL

When a man, who claims to have the moral right to freedom of expression, is a liar, a prostitute, whose political judgments can be bought, a dishonest creator of hates and suspicions, his affirmation is illegitimate and unfruitful. From the moral point of view, at least, liberty of expression does not include the right to lie, as a deliberate instrument of a policy.

> —Report of the North American Commission on Freedom of the Press (1947). Presided over by the Rector of the University of Chicago, Dr. Hutchins [Retranslated from the Spanish]

The anti-Communist psychosis . . . has as one of its objectives that of preparing conditions for the destruction

of the struggles of the peoples for
national liberation.
—Confederación de Trabajadores
de la América Latina. Mexico,
1952

The Police Rulers exercise a *structural* anti-Kommunism. That is to say, it corresponds to the anatomy and
physiology of this type of government, and serves splen-
didly to protect it and strengthen it, tending to prolong
and perpetuate the regime. The North American industrialists package and ship out a different kind of anti-
Kommunism, but equally organic; since it properly serves
their commercial calculations—the reason for existence of
the great incorporated enterprise known as the United
States of America. The Catholic Church, for its part,
predicates a third type of anti-Kommunism, more sophisti-
cated, more demonstrative, which answers perfectly the
need to recover positions lost in the material and mundane, in political influence and commercial relations; the
need to augment its financial resources, its desire to recover its monopoly on the spiritual formation of children
and youths. These three kinds of anti-Kommunism are
long-lasting, to the degree to which social evolution allows
them to exist. They are serviceable and long-lived for each
of these politico-social entities known as the dictators, the
millionaires, and the Church. And they will be even more
enduring now that these three factories of anti-Kommunism have celebrated a diabolic alliance which makes them
sisters in the grand task: first to slow up, then destroy the
march of democratic principles; to wipe out the liberal

spirit that inspires contemporary social life and smash down every little expression of "personality" in the ordinary man.

But there are many other sources of anti-Kommunism, anti-Kommunism not so enduring. These feed anti-Kommunism according to circumstances: at any given moment can suspend production. Notable for example is the anti-Kommunism of publicity experts. They offer their services to keep artificial fires burning, to multiply the surface hullabaloo, to distract the attention of those who wish to reason or to investigate; to collect what can be called "garbage" and burn incense at the feet of those who are to be accepted as gods; to mount the bell-towers a few minutes before mass or a little after the funeral procession goes by; to provide the uniforms, the street insignias, the luminous torches; they proceed to capture and torture the victim, giving him the *tiro de gracia* (the last shot in the head in the hour of grace) and then bury him in a Christian manner or cremate him while he is still warm. These are the "Geese of the Capitol," about which a delicious legend has been told, how they are quick to give their short, strong cackle to warn that the barbarians are coming, the new people, the enemies of the Latin flock: zoological, elementary and unconscious zoological contributions, which favor one band in the age-old dispute born of the desires of the plebes to live a little better, a little longer.

The best cackles come from the big newspapers, the industrialized press, press of the millionaires for selected readers. Their contribution is a noisy one. But their anti-Kommunism is not functional. Publicity experts move with divergent, even contradictory, purposes. Their ideological points of view are artificial, changeable, provisional. In this hour of the world and on this continent, they also bring forth anti-Kommunism at the behest of the affluent.

Disguised by concern for public welfare enterprises, the big press penetrates all homes, inspires confidence, entertains the adults and enchants the children. The parents have no idea how many slimy matters crawl through the funnies, underneath the moralizing editorials, alongside the poems about springtime. The universal fiction that the big newspapers are meant to serve social interests, culture, health, and morality is naively accepted. It costs much effort and sorrow to be able to discover, behind the fiction, the terrible reality.

In its editorial column of January 20, 1925, the *Wall Street Journal* remarked: "A daily is a private enterprise, which owes nothing to the public, to which it concedes no rights. As a result, it is not tied up with any public interest. It is, emphatically, the property of its owner, who sells a product manufactured at his own risk." "The manager [of a paper] actually is subject to the corrections or suggestions of the owner, who considers it simply a business."[1]

Here is the baptismal certificate of contemporary journalism. Journalism of millionaires, who supplant and bury the journalism of journalists. Journalism today is business; and a business, by definition, is the search for the biggest profits in the quickest time by whatever means. Everything else is thrown away under the desks or into the waste basket. By simple coincidence in that year of 1925 there died one of the archetypes of this supercapitalist

169

journalism. A compatriot and colleague of the defunct, from Emporia, Kansas, wrote the following epitaph:

> Frank Munsey, famous owner of newspapers, has died. Frank Munsey brought to the journalism of his times the talent of an owner of refrigerator plants, the morals of a money-changer, and the habits of a mortician. He and the ones who aided him succeeded in transforming what in another epoch was a noble profession into a business with a margin of return of eight percent. May he rest in peace.[2]

A journalism managed in this manner is just one industry more which returns dividends similar to those that are returned by capital invested in oil wells, for example. Nevertheless, we are obliged to continue calling it journalism. This new industry owns property registered in commercial activity: trucks, automobiles, houses, bank deposits, linotypes, presses, paper, ink, lead, newspaper men, typewriters, reporters, photographers, artists, caricaturists. More recently, loudspeakers, microphones, and television screens have been added.

To these physical and human assets, we add a juridical property: the right to inform. Not the duty to inform, but the right. This right also is "sacred," as we shall see presently. Contemporary publicity has its own requirements as a business, and its own morality. All the managing and editorial personnel should obey the owner or owners meeting as directors. The paper "now" has an idea, a line to follow. More than one United States daily has imposed the "oath of loyalty" to this thought, this line.

170

Thus the right of providing information is the right of the owner, a right which for editors is transformed into the duty of thinking the same as the owner. And the owner thinks day and night of the prosperity of his business. It is a thought of calculation. It is a thought that becomes an obsession—the obsession of eight percent. The ideal of the newspaper owner is to convert the reader into a buyer. Not a buyer of his periodical but a buyer of the merchandise which is advertised in the paper. Very well, but the manufacturers of this merchandise are also multimillionaires, and the newspaper should publish in favor of the social system of the millionaires. Simple. Very simple. Now the owner no longer has the right to inform; he has the duty to give the information which the millionaires wish him to give.

Thus was born the journalistic thesis about the "defense of society," understood as a commercial society, an accumulation of capital. Thus was born the anti-Kommunism of the newspaper men, which is the same as that of the millionaires, which in turn is nothing more than the anti-Kommunism of the Department of State.

* * *

There was an epoch, however, in which the new journalistic industry and the Department of State were unable to understand each other. This was during the presidency of Franklin Delano Roosevelt. The New Deal, the Wagner Act, the new banking law, supervision of transportation, changes in the Supreme Court, new taxes, investigation of monopolies, the National Recovery Act, the Tennessee

Valley hydroelectric project, labor union freedom, the official anti-Nazi climate—all this indicated to the newsmen that the new style of the Department of State "betrayed" the best and most honest ambitions of the super-capitalists. From that time most government functionaries became "agents in the pay of Moscow" as also were Congressmen, the Supreme Court judges, the heads of the governing party. Even President Roosevelt received his pay in rubles. If this expression "agents in the pay of Moscow" had a date it also had its author who coined it and propagated it throughout the entire country, with the cunning of a publicity technician, with the passion of a capitalist defending his wealth, with the vehemence of one playing with destiny. This extraordinary man was a speculator in oil (we have said millionaire) who, subsidized by oil, etc., had purchased one by one various important dailies until he put together a chain of dailies in the country. This symbolic man was William Randolph Hearst. From the very beginning of that chain, the Hearst school spoke of freedom. Freedom of expression, independence of the newspaper man, liberty of access to the sources of news, such were the first assignments of the flag in the fight. Journalism went from a business to the university and from the university to the pulpit. The language was carried to the lofty point of speaking of the "sacred virtues of the press and the sanctity of telegraphic cables." The pedagogue and the mystic served as the air-supplied suits for a few deep-sea divers.

To Hearst's misfortune, the new order installed in the United States by Franklin Delano Roosevelt was not propitious for the plans and stratagems of sacerdotal journal-

172

ism. In the year 1936, when the first presidential term of
Roosevelt ended, a battle was joined to decide whether
the United States would at last set up a Nazi-fascist-type
dictatorship or whether it preferred leftist type democracy
by reelecting Roosevelt. Mister Hearst and his scholars
bet some millions against the president, along with their
prestige as great industrialists of news gathering and as
efficacious conductors of public opinion. However, it did
not seem intelligent to defend Hitler without knowing
him, and Mister Hearst went in person to Germany to
feel out and admire at first hand the work of that Messiah,
spokesman for a god and a race. Hearst returned to the
United States, rich in reasons and documents. That was
when the functionaries of the Department of State became
"agents in the pay of Moscow." The President of the
United States became a vulgar traitor to the nation.

But in all this could be observed something more than
proselytizing passion or ideological devotion. It had to do
with a desperate personal defense. Roosevelt and his subalterns and the authentic press (which still existed in the
country) had discovered and were showing up the trickery
of the Hearst periodical empire and the obscure under-
ground dens where "the boys" worked. For its part, the
leaders of North American dailies themselves severely
condemned that industrial-style journalism which at a
given moment could boast of "making presidents." Workers, organizations, university professors, independent politicians, journalists with a liberal mentality, church congre-
gations, and high functionaries of justice joined to fight
collectively against venal journalism which promoted the
Hitler ideological line on this side of the Atlantic, those

who until 1944 had exalted the "good dictatorship" of Mussolini. The same ones who a few months later demanded the military invasion of Mexico!

What was the nature of this science of news and this *journalistic technique* practiced with such success by Hearst and his kind? Like every new science it consisted of very elementary things: Manufacture news and sell it as authentic; deform true news, partly or wholly falsify it; mutilate it by publishing excerpts; transform calumny into news and deny the person so smeared the right of self-defense; rewrite the news by introducing strange ingredients; postpone publication until the news lost its significance; "interpret" the news according to whimsical self-interest; "bury" important items, by losing them purposely among business advertisements; bar publication of certain reports; alter the news sent in by correspondents abroad, without advising them; attribute to persons declarations they never made; put quotation marks about some important phrase, thus pretending it was supplied by written text; falsify the headlines to make them say something different from the articles themselves, etc., etc. As another distinguished newspaper man, Mr. Howard [*World Telegram*] has also defined journalism as the art of "selling news," the one conclusion that the intelligent public can draw is that Mr. Hearst and his imitators were selling false news in return for legitimate money, a stunt that in any penal code is known as—fraud, and fraud is punishable by jailing.

Also it was proved that they were giving preference to the sale of "space" for the advertising of spurious foods, fictitious and harmful medicines, magical cure-alls, creams for restoring youth, unhealthful cigarettes, "Scotch"

174

whiskys made in the Dakotas, and other marvels of small industry, or big industry, and that they never published the scientific exposures of the bad quality of such products, thus perpetrating a double fraud and criminal complicity. It was further proved that they also practiced extortion to secure advertisements, and on explicit occasions this Pleiades of publicity experts had gone so far as to practice blackmail, demanding lush "bribes" (*mordidas*) in return for keeping silent. *Silence!* The space most productive in publicity matters! From small, occasional, innocuous silences, the press comes in due time to organize real "conspiracies" of silence against any given affair of public interest. Silences which favor, naturally, its generous advertisers.

To this must be added that the powerful Associated Press (representative of other supercapitalistic sectors) was able to show in a common court that Mister Hearst practiced a certain type of corrupt practices known as *bribery;* for he obtained news by improper means, paying off the telegraphers of other concerns. To this we add the most infantile and most hoary of tricks: the *New York Post* accused him of fabricating "documents" and turning out "cosmographs" or false composite photographs. We remember, finally, that some of Mr. Hearst's shameful professional activities, on a certain occasion, won him the honor of being expelled from French soil.[3]

These, precisely, are the journalists who were brazen enough to write out a "Code of Ethics" and to set forth a "Decalogue of the Journalist." We do not know why they needed this. Perhaps it is only another disguise. Because there we encounter the pious concept that forbids the seller of news to disclose the source of his information.

175

This marvelous precept, translated into ordinary language, merely means: "freedom to calumniate." Another professional victory in the new code, provides that no industrialists or merchant of news can be denied the right to print or use "private" or "confidential" documents.[4] Already, quite apart from the code, the news enterprises oblige writers to maintain a constant false pretense of opinions; the underling must think exactly as does the manager; the latter, as the owners; and the owners as do the advertisers. Otherwise they would lose their jobs or the advertisements. A fantastic mode of conduct in those who cry out (from the door of the house to passers-by) in favor of "freedom of expression" and respect for the independence of the newsman.

Ultramodern dailies also compete for priority of *news;* they pay those who have it to offer; if there are no offers, they are sought out, and if none are discovered, the news is fabricated. To accomplish this, correspondents are sent to the places where events interesting to the public (those most in demand) are occurring or where they are about to occur. The correspondents follow instructions from New York or Chicago and fly madly from one country to another. Thus when disturbances begin in Algeria, death by ambush becomes news. The news enterprises, journalists, and newsreel photographers (all the same thing) want to offer the fact of death in the exact instant it occurs. The North American public has to see, has "to be present" in person, as it is said, at the terrible instant in which a French soldier or a native Algerian falls wounded to death or is burned alive. (The Algerian victim comes cheaper.) And so, for example: Fox Movietone News performed a miracle! Their Algerian correspondent, George Chassagne, was accused by the French government of bribing a French gendarme to shoot an inoffensive musulman so as to provide news by means of this tragic device. Fox Movietone has not been the only publicity enterprise to pay for such luxury.[5] The "Code of Ethics" of this journalism of the atomic age found nothing to criticize in the case of Chassagne. The French tribunals didn't want to complicate things either!

At the same time that the "Tablet of Commandments" of this singular business, heralded as the defender of the public good, was perfected, Mr. Hearst and his boys, to oppose the new policies of Roosevelt, calumniated union organizations, used spies in the editorial staff and in his own shops, organized and paid criminal strikebreakers, humiliated his employees and workers, proclaimed the virtues of war (whenever Roosevelt talked of peace), was pacifist (when Roosevelt no longer favored peace), exalted the ideas and work of Hitler and Mussolini, fought all forms of pure democracy, reviled public functionaries, poked into the private lives of his adversaries, "bought" the journalists of rival dailies.

Because of all this, the urgent need was felt to set a limit, to bring such methods, such men, and that unique code of ethics, to the bar of public opinion. These were the same days that a multimillionaire, J. P. Morgan, was seated on the bench of the accused because of the suspicion that "his interests" had pushed the United States into World War I. Millions of Yankees died, it was believed, to save the many billions Morgan had invested in Europe. Hearst and his boys were also taken before a people's tribunal in which even religious confessions were given. Thousands attended the sessions. This tribunal declared

Hearst a "traitor to the United States." Three presidents of the nation felt it necessary to publicly repudiate this murky personage and his newspapers. Senator Minton accused him of "prostituting freedom of the press." According to Senator Schwellenbach "all decent newspaper owners had been enemies of Hearst ever since 1895. . . ." This same Senator mentioned Hearst as an accomplice in the assassination of President McKinley. "Never has any man exercised such destructive and immoral influence to drag down to the depths the supreme ideals which defend all religious institutions as has William Randolph Hearst," said the Ministers' Social Action organization of New York. Finally New York's governor, Alfred Smith, called him "a plague walking in the dark."

And so this personage, in order to defend himself from public and official wrath, and as revenge for defeat in his campaign against the first re-election of Roosevelt, decided and so ordered that henceforth all adversaries should be tagged with the brief incisive phrase "agents in the pay of Moscow." Even President Roosevelt merited the singular descriptive epithet, "foreign agitator." Naturally "agents in the pay of Moscow" were those persons who did not enlist in the current world-saving crusade of Nazi-Fascism which in those moments was prospering in Europe. Even the "Federal Council of Churches of Christ" merited this "agents of Moscow" epithet, hurled by Hearst himself.

All this makes us recall that in the same year of 1936, a half dozen Spanish Generals on a Mediterranean island started their crusade for Christianity, aimed first of all at sweeping out of Spain all democratic spirit. They carried the banner of anti-Kommunism. Hitler and Mussolini— those very same mentors of Hearst—were the financiers and suppliers of the anti-Spanish military enterprise. From the very first moment, "Agents in the pay of Moscow" were the heads of the Spanish government and everybody who fought to defend the Republic.

The designation, naturally, had European origin, the trademark of the Fascists, undeniably, inseparably linked with the industrialists and capitalists on both sides of the Atlantic. "Agents in the pay of Moscow," "spies of the Russians" exactly as Hitler had set forth in his bible of anti-Kommunism, *Mein Kampf*. "A parade of Communists always looks like a parade of Jews," George Sokolsky, colleague of Hearst and commissioned by the makers of steel, sympathizers and "arms-suppliers" of the armies of Hitler, had written.

*　*　*

The high authority of the "school" of journalism and the ethical code of Mr. Hearst did not remain there in the north to become another facet of the North American way of life. Because of the general tendency of our time, they could not resign themselves to carrying on this battle merely for the benefit of native Yankees or the immigrants who adopted English as their own language. They had to offer this slab of salvation to their little Latin brothers to the south. They thought about it, they plotted it, and they succeeded.

At the present time, the big Latin American press responds to the same supercapitalist structure as does the big press of the United States. The commercial spirit and the financial methods—the international banking system —already have penetrated into the world of journalism, once upon a time proletarian. The tie-ups with the re-

179

maining wheels of the industrial system have also been made. In 1948 in Montevideo at the request of the United Nations, a poll was taken concerning freedom of the press. The replies provided conclusions sufficient to demonstrate that South America, too, was already suffering from the new industrial system known in the United States as "journalism." The poll was organized and evaluated by the Uruguayan Press Association.

The theory that defines journalism as the art of manufacturing and selling news and the revolutionary concept that the news is a free personal speculation, have been integrated with the "professional" doings of industry journalists. Already the Yankee influence has advanced to the point of convincing us that this moralizing missionary type of journalism is at the center of cultural life and has become the support of the essential liberties of man, among which is freedom of expression. But freedom to express oneself and freedom of the press thereupon become synonymous. And in the end, freedom to publish has been fused with the absolute freedom of those who manufacture the elements necessary to publish: linotypes and paper, for example. But this is not the whole of this confusion of duties, ideas, and utilities. There would come a moment—and it has come—in which the freedom to publish and to inform, which is arrogated by the millionaires, is insidiously merged with the desires of the innocent readers of newspapers, whereupon the rights of the industrialists are understood to be those of everybody: the interchangeable right of informing and being informed; and the interchangeable right of selling any news and of buying any news. At this point, the right of publishing becomes something intangible for it has been transformed magically into "the right of the people to inform themselves freely," according to *El Mercurio*, Santiago de Chile, January 9, 1958. We recall also that Pan Americanism—another imperialist instrument—at the beginning was a simple machine in the hands of governments; but since 1947 in treaties it came to be spoken of as the hope or the ideal "of the people." This topic is discussed in Chapter III of my book, *The Shark and the Sardines*.

As a result this journalism is no longer the voice of millionaires, entrepreneurs, investors, stock speculators, manipulators of the international market: no, this sort of journalism has become the expression of the people's soul, the soul of the peoples who thus provide themselves, in unlimited freedom, with the news they need. A bit later we will be told about "the sacred right of the people to accept as being of divine origin everything that the holy industrialists wish to tell us: the holy industrialists who manufacture linotypes, paper, and printer's ink."

* * *

Not only industrialized, supercapitalized and blessed with holy water, the Big-Big Press of Latin America has also been *internationalized*. Here young students of journalism can find a fertile theme for investigation. To what extent have the big dailies in our countries abandoned their old-time patriotic ideas and replaced them with obligations to foreign oligarchies? In other words: how and when have they made the transition from predicating in behalf of the interests of the country to that of favoring a powerful competitive domineering country? There are the editorials; there are the "columnists;" there

181

are the recent collaborators. Any student of the history of journalism will find, to his sorrow or his fury, proof that the boundaries of the fatherland, "*the patria*," have been extended to continental limits beyond the people, the language, the religion, the native traditions, and the advice bequeathed to us by the great leaders of the last century. Far beyond the Constitution of the Republics! The big press says it has quit being "chauvinist," it no longer feels superpatriotic, not provincial nor cheaply petty. Generosity is the passion that now characterizes and orients the press: that of giving itself "to the big neighbor" and "giving all."

Undoubtedly this internationalization has led to a reorientation of the big press or, better said, a certain disorientation with respect to old nationalist themes, one with more elevated broader outlook. The political ideas of the journalists of our big press are now "continental" ideas; they think on a hemispheric scale. The matter is serious for, to the extent these superjournalists adopt as their own the continental or hemispheric "outlook," they lose contact with their fellow countrymen. What is being attempted is the conversion of the big press into a new political organism, badly disguised, which operates according to the formulas of the international system. What is being attempted is the formation of a new political party, a local cell, with fraternal relations, that represent a leveling and an absorption which the old-style political parties would be ashamed to defend. The matter deals with political voices which speak in the name of politicians over there, which say here now what those over there wish to have said here, now; which say what native politicians, the professional politicians, would refuse to say. They are the defenders of international interests that cannot be defended, except in this moralistic well-codified tribunal of the disciples of Hearst.

Supercapitalized, industrialized, blessed with holy water, internationalized and brainwashed, this big press at the same time has been monopolized. Not in the economic sense, but profession-wise in everything in which journalism should display its daily pride: monopolized through the distribution of news. There are three hemispheric organizations which manufacture and sell world news: the United Press of the Scripps-Howard family, the International News Service of Mr. Hearst and his heirs, and the Associated Press. The first two named merged in the middle of 1958, thereby being converted into the "intellectual" antenna of the financial and industrial interests which we know by the name of the House of Morgan. The Associated Press is the "intellectual" antenna of the powerful political bloc known in the United States as the "National Association of Newspaper Publishers," a publicity instrument at the same time of the succulent maternal "National Association of Manufacturers" in which the House of Morgan also operates surreptitiously. We are therefore faced by what is universally called a monopoly. A monopoly of world news subject to the monopoly of North American industrialists. And at once the reader can imagine what remarkable interest the Manufacturers' Association has in nature, intent, and purpose of the news it buys, evaluates, edits, sells, and distributes. The great dailies of Latin America cannot complain. They buy from the National Association of Manufacturers fresh news with telephotos of all hot events, and they sell them, they resell them unaltered, intact, to the readers of Latin America. Latin, to be sure was a news

183

agency that operated with Argentine and Brazilian capital. The poor little fellow could not grow. His news was of inferior quality. It responded to regional interests and spoke of nationalism. Its antennas were short, lacking sensitivity, incapable of penetrating into the secrets of our times. In addition, the agency had a quixotic note and tried to revive the journalistic methods of last century. It disseminated news that might have discredited the United States. And it collapsed. France Presse and Reuters are two European agencies which are still permitted to sell news in this hemisphere. But they will not be tolerated for many more years.

Monopolized and (we would prefer not to say this) subsidized is our Big Press. The concept of subsidies is of official origin and nationalist significance. An assistance, subsidies are funds that a government grants to agricultural or industrial enterprises that perform services in the national interest, when such enterprises fall into economic difficulties. But in the case of the big North American press, the subvention has not been by the government. The powerful industrialists are these who grant the subsidies. It is publicly known, for example, that toward the end of 1946 the National Electric Light Association of the United States was spending $25,000,000 annually to advertise and thereby influence the daily papers, the columnists and reporters. It boasted of having at its feet 80 percent of the Yankee press. Up to two billion dollars is the budget which the great industrial corporations in the United States have for confidential handling of the noble newsmen of the Hearst "school." Merely in the year 1937, the National Association of Manufacturers invested at least $3,000,000 in this task of reeducation.

Since that date, the figure may have been doubled.[6] An honorable example: The magazine *Saturday Evening Post* was favored by $50,000 from a single firm: National Electric. In the way of fiscal subsidies to the Big Yankee Press, we are justified in supposing that the quantities are equally generous. Thus, like the paleontologists who, on discovering a fossil, are able, by imagination mixed with science, to reconstruct from it the entire skeleton, so we can imagine "mathematically" the orgy of dollars which stimulated the Jove-thundering moralists of journalism. For example we have here a transatlantic "bone" which helps us reconstruct the entire skeleton: the Spanish Agency, Agencia Española, which operates in the democratic orbit of France, received from the United States budget a subsidy which around 1954 totaled $391,000. With what good reason, the Falangist (Fascist) chatter favors the free world[7] from cities and "villas" such as in Madrid, Barcelona, Valencia, Bilbao and Sevilla. And still another bone: From the city of Munich, Nazi chatter in Hitleresque Germany—from 188 functionaries and employees, who operate under the name of "Voice of America" and receive salaries from Washington.[8]

We do not put ourselves, even so, on the level of the scrupulous religious female fanatic if we come to discover that the big Latin American press also, as garrulous as that of Franco and the neo-Hitlerites, receives subsidies in six or seven figures. Aside from some Ambassadorial bank checks,[9] which by negligence have come to light "in a Latin desk," there are the commercial advertisements paid for per millimeter in gold, which cease to be purchased as soon as the daily makes a mistake; also the resounding and constant contributions to the anti-Kommu-

185

nist "crusade"—such are the diplomatic and distorted cultural methods of subsidy. Then there are the scholarships for advanced instruction in the schools of the United States granted directly by the State Department or directly (!) by industrial concerns: sumptuous vacation trips to "improve" relations, decorating with medals of "merit," unlimited dollars, etc., etc.

When journalists in the United States (it cannot be hidden very long) became aware of this system of protecting the newspaper industry and the industrious newsmen, Professor T. V. Smith, of the philosophy department of the University of Chicago, exploded against such elements: he called them *"plutogogues"* i.e. spokesmen for the plutocrats, also "elegant lackeys"—euphemistic expressions that have come to replace others still harsher with which the public in the United States had been abusing them. We are not so cruel in Latin America.

Our delightful commentators, when they are promoted to the offices of these dailies subsidized by a foreign power or foreign enterprise, never cease to be newspaper men. On the contrary they are the proudest ones of their profession: they are the ones chosen to give lectures in any "school of journalism" connected with the universities.

We are not surprised, therefore, that all our big newspapers are anti-Kommunist, indefatigable gladiators in the arena where the destinies of the free world are at stake: the rights of man, of western civilization, freedom of opportunity, and all the rest. But we should not be the least surprised that when issues are debated in which native interests cannot be reconciled with the interests of the Empire, these aristocrats of journalism use the golden prestige of their pens to favor the foreign point of view.

186

In an editorial in a major Santiago de Chile newspaper, I read a defense of the United States when in 1953 the fellow citizens of O'Higgins protested against the low prices fixed for copper in international "markets." When Chile, Peru, and Ecuador decided to extend their sovereignty over coastal waters, out to two hundred miles, this same paper . . . Chilean . . . in an April 9, 1956, editorial, again justified the adverse position taken by the United States. When in 1956 the Arabs threatened to destroy the oil pipelines during the Suez Canal crisis, another big Chilean daily, believing that England and France would perish from hunger, came out editorially offering as compensation . . . the oil of Chile.

Let us jump abruptly from the land of Chile to Uruguay. Latin Americans had been protesting at the injury inflicted on the local economy by the United States in dumping its farm surpluses. On August 16, 1958, a leading Montevideo daily came out aggressively in its editorial column in defense of the United States, which, it was stated, could not halt "such disposal of its farm surpluses for to do so would depress its production." Also, the editor argued, there is a law—(Law of the Empire, No. 480) which provides for such dumping. As a result, he continued, what Uruguay must do is reorient its economy, producing only goods that will not disturb the exports of the Colossus.

We continue in Montevideo. (It is not humanly possible to present documents from all the Latin American capitals. I have merely taken these rosebud boutonnieres from the dailies which I myself habitually read in the cities where I resided.) As a result of the clamorous reception which Latin American students accorded Vice-Presi-

187

dent Nixon (April and May, 1958) the Department of State pretended that *"only lately"* had it become aware of the existence of such a popular attitude. The President of Brazil used this as a pretext to promote meetings to investigate the causes of youthful rebellion and correct conditions.[10] With . . . Marxist . . . simplicity, they were ascribed to the economic difficulties which the southern countries were suffering. And as a result of the scandal, money—much money—was promised to create a sympathetic attitude . . . in the universities. The uproar having abated, spirits having cooled off, six months later "The 21" met in the capital of the Empire, and the United States resumed its invariable evasions. The Latin American delegates, even the most obsequious ones, were insubordinate. The Brazilian delegate took the lead. He was followed by the Bolivian delegate. At this juncture, the ever-loyal Uruguayan daily resumed its mysterious defense of the United States. It jeered cruelly at "Latin American rhetoric" and eulogized the Yankee spirit of pragmatism. The United States, the *South American* editorial said, has no obligation to support lazy people. "This is the epoch of men of action." The United States—land of practical people—is not amused by these melodramas of the eternally lazy southlanders.

We have presented the testimony of typical editorials, already archived in dim libraries for the pleasure of students of history and journalism and, as the saying goes, of "foreign" influences. Unfortunately here, as in the case of presidential discourses, it is not easy to know *who is the author*. Nor is it even possible to affirm that the editorials were originally written in Spanish. A deep suspicion, which turns inside us day and night, tries to get at the

188

many varied methods of the Empire. Aided by idiomatic clues, we have become convinced that some of these literary pieces were originally written in English. Once they are translated into Spanish, the Embassy functionary who feeds the "patriotic" fire, writes on them in his own hand the implacable order "Publish."

There is no need to resort to the imagination. The Uruguayan students in their paper *Jornada,* Montevideo, May 17, 1956, exposed the little *gaffe* perpetrated by the great Uruguay daily *El Plata,* when on March 21 it printed what allegedly was its own report, the text, word for word without changes, of a loose-leaf bulletin distributed by the U.S. Information Service, a police cell annexed to the Embassies of the Empire. [In many cities in Latin America, I was informed that representatives of the Information Service call periodically on the important editors to inquire why such and such bulletins were not utilized. This official propaganda, masquerading as news, is so distorted, false, biased, and in the case of Cuba and the Soviet Union, so downright vicious, that many editors, though anxious to oblige, simply dare not print much of it lest the good name of their newspaper be tarnished and they themselves be placed in ridicule.—Translator]

This sort of translation from one language to the other, like that spiritual distortion of what is local to what is hemispheric, appeared years ago, as a privilege of peoples who live beneath the musical echoes of the Caribbean. In my first book in this polemical series, *Guatemala, Democracy and the Empire,* I spoke of the bilingual Presidents, who travel to the United States to render accounts, provide explanations, or to beg; also the presidential candidates who "go up" to Washington to give

189

guarantees of loyalty and who carry on part of their "electoral" propaganda on Yankee soil. This Caribbean sea, to which I dedicated lyrical and sorrowing pages, now reaches to Arequipa, Peru. Since 1954, a tragic year (and not merely tragic for Guatemala), the Caribbean Sea has grown and its symbolic waters filter far south and overflow forests and pampas and become mingled with the wide Plata River, blood brother to be sure. Now the bilingualism (idiomatic and mental) has become interpolated, throughout the hemisphere, thanks to the transformation of the big press and those Embassies with which it works in unison.

Uruguay's experience in these directions is painful. In Montevideo definite proof has been provided. The two large papers of the capital were obliged under duress of the bitter reality to publish as an editorial the same article received from outside.

* * *

When I came to the River Plata the first time, I enjoyed the public tribute which *La Nación* and *La Prensa* of Buenos Aires provided in its Sunday supplements. The great and sonorous Leopoldo Lugones flourished his pen, sharpened in classical learning, and taught his critics perfect Spanish. Arturo Capdevila, profound and picaresque, led the Babel of immigrants along the highways of Hispanicism. With them, beside them or behind them, audacious essayists, inspired poets, men of science, historians, philosophers, art specialists provided a spiritual feast! The tradition came from many years back; the end of the last century. Perhaps Sarmiento and Mitre, [two of

190

Argentina's greatest presidents, thinkers, and authors]
were the forerunners. It was also the epoch of outside
geniuses: Rubén Darío, who spilled out his poetry along
the Calle Florida; José Martí, who shouted his sorrows
from the United States. And it was also the epoch of that
other great stranger (not really a foreigner) named Paul
Groussac, a distinguished Frenchman who came to write
Castilian as though it were his maternal tongue. And, a
little later, the Guatemalan Enrique Gómez Carrillo, who
commanded both Castilian and French with a talent similar to that of Groussac. Such was the breed which pushed
back the petty and the infantile. And so it was I listened
to the collaborators of the two greatest literary tribunes
of South American journalism.

But there is no human greatness that is not vulnerable
and, by 1928, the two papers had acquired such a mutual
aversion that neither would admit the existence of the
other. And, add a petty rumor: it was told to me that a
writer who collaborated for one of the papers found the
doors of the other closed to him. As is customary in such
cases, only original unpublished contributions became the
rule, no reprints. Two hired provincial poets from Córdoba
led the contest for beauty and glory.

Imagine then my surprise when, at the beginning of
1957, I observed that both papers printed the work of a
foreign collaborator until then unknown as a writer, and
above all unknown in Spanish, perhaps the only one who
had ever broken the severe norms of *La Nación* and *La
Prensa*. In this instance to which I refer, the high literary
quality was lost, and for the first time the two dailies
accepted the same atrocious collaborator. Still another
concession: the two dailies published the same article

without the slightest variation. But even worse: the article, which both of the proud Río Plata dailies were offering its readers, was the same that had been previously published during the days of January and February in various Latin American capitals. A mimeographed article eulogizing Castillo Armas! The mystery began to be cleared up when it appeared that this revolutionary collaboration had been sent from the United States by King Features Syndicate, Inc., against which indications the two big Argentine dailies had no defensive argument.

And who is this writer who in this manner offended the South American tradition? He was Colonel Jules Dubois. Not precisely a man of war nor an aesthete either. Humbly the Colonel presented himself as a journalist. But he is not that either. He could, perhaps, present himself as a newspaper proprietor. But not even this. Perhaps only a stockholder, with a small or large part of the profits produced by the most isolationist of the North American dailies, the *Chicago Tribune*.[11]

One is a bit surprised that his army status is injected among literary people; we pacify our uneasiness by recalling that General Mitre, founder of *La Nación,* was an outstanding historian and a translator of Dante. At least in *La Nación,* the new collaborator could bow in smiling. And if we believe that Capdevila may be the deciding voice in *La Prensa,* we cannot forget that the grandeur of his spirit as a poet makes him able to accept at his side a colleague of this sort; it would be impossible to say that he suffers from racial prejudices. But the matter is complicated when we know that Jules is not French but North American. On one good occasion, we said that his literary wood would be burgeoning in the name ("of the forest")

192

with its memories of a dormer window view. But no: Colonel Jules Dubois is a gentleman of the skyscrapers, there in the heart of Chicago.

Our personage is one of the greatest authorities of the Inter-American Press Society (SIP). For ten years he presided over the Committee for A Free Press. This, let us note, is a society of owners of newspapers, a trade union or syndicate of owners of dailies, a syndicate of millionaires. As proprietors of the newspaper industry, they engaged in the humanitarian task of defending free enterprise, in this instance the enterprise of publishing: almost, almost also freedom of opinion; that, for example, of Mr. Hearst. But at the same time, they defend the profits, legitimate or not, of property, holy or not. They defend a social order instituted centuries ago. And also its modern habits. Above all they defend the freedom to fabricate and sell news. That is why the syndicate looks at the world from the viewpoint of business, and they call themselves journalists only in so far as they are "owners" of publishing enterprises or are at the service of those owners. They are the investors in journalism. They are, within journalism, a fraternity of financiers. It is the same Association of Newspaper Proprietors of the United States, but in its inter-American guise it is shaped by the export trade, i.e., the importation of dollars paid out for machinery, paper, information, services. With this syndicate (SIP) are always present the other enterprises we have mentioned: UP, INS, AP. They are birds of a feather; and the plumage of all of them is bilingual. They speak Spanish and write it. They learned the language, as Milton Eisenhower, the brother of brothers, learned it on his first tour of South America; they learned it from disks and practiced it in night clubs, and they write it whenever they have at hand a Puerto Rican to correct the syntax.

There is the road, the truth, and the life. There is the road that runs from the lightning flashes of the bank offices of New York to the obscure pages of the two squeamish Spanish-language dailies. There is the road traversed by this new collaborator, whom, were it not for this disclosure, anybody might suppose is of the same caliber as Paul Groussac. But no, neither in style nor in political ideas. Because Dubois is the most complete example of anti-Kommunism in our days, whereas Groussac, there in 1880, was one of the precursors of the Kommunism of today. And right off here we have room for a new investigation of the history of journalism: of Río Plata journalism. It would have as its theme "foreign" influences. First, the Caribbean influence: José Martí, Rubén Darío, Enrique Goméz Carillo, Maximo Soto Hall. The influence of the French Kommunists: Groussac. Finally the Biblical North American anti-Kommunist influence: Jules Dubois. And to crown these proofs of the investigation: we propose a transatlantic title: "From Paul Groussac to Jules Dubois."

For there are golden threads that serve to guide us through this labyrinth of ideas, to identify what seem to be ideas and strip off the vegetable parasites hanging onto ideas. History tells us, for example, that when José Martí sent his contributions to *La Nación,* the editor of the day in Buenos Aires crossed out some of the phrases of the Cuban apostle and stylist, who had seen the claws of the imperial eagle, close at hand. "Don't forget that a newspaper is a property," Bartolome Mitre y Vedia, in the name of the family, explained to him. And Martí, who served a continental cause, as does Jules Dubois, but completely opposite that of the pseudo-Frenchman, allowed himself to be corrected from Buenos Aires, because . . . even then it was not "commercial" to point out the true facts or prognosticate future aggressions by the United States.[12] To reconcile commercialism with ideology ever since then has been a difficult task for Río Plata journalism. Disgracefully, too, ever since those days, commercialism has been gaining big profits from that reconciliation. Men of vigorous thought like Martí have had to tone down their inspiration or else renounce journalism, thus opening the way for a new crowd of which Jules Dubois is the prototype. Who would dare either in *La Nación* or *La Prensa* so much as correct a single phrase of the United Fruit propagandist, Jules Dubois? A fine stylist like Martí —anybody corrects him. In the last analysis, he was paid a few pesos and should be thankful. Jules Dubois, in contrast, is not one who is paid; he is on the side of those who pay.

But let us come back to SIP. We were noting that it is a syndicate of millionaires. Set up to defend the investments of the industrialists of the press throughout the hemisphere, it has forged a far-flung strong chain of interests weighted with political power. It represents six hundred directors and newspaper sidekickers—i.e., so-called journalists who are alert day and night to the winds that blow through the stock exchange. The joking of the investment business and the news-gathering trade has brought to this little world what we know as "literary people." The newspaper people and intellectuals resemble each other in this; both groups are "people of letters." There is, therefore, a bridge by which the owner of the enterprise or a business administrator crosses over easily

195

from the calculation of dividends and free customs duties, to the library and from there to the study hall, reserved for those who investigate and create. This bridge of gold and smoke has been traveled by the new writer of Spanish, the incorrigible Colonel Jules Dubois. Once he reaches the study hall, the Colonel sits down and . . . gives orders. He is the most brilliant disciple of Mr. Hearst. He is Mr. Hearst brought up to date; for Dubois travels, goes forth from the confines of the metropolis, and visits and inspects the Provinces. Every time business runs any risk, Dubois, the guardian angel, flies down to look and to solve it. He speaks with the authority he enjoys as "president" and he brings with him the holy decalogue of the contemporary journalist. The international fame of his newspaper, the *Chicago Tribune,* no longer throws any shadow on him. The memory of Mr. Hearst and Herr Hitler has long since vanished. But what has not vanished is the English which slinks in among the Spanish syllables. He does not conceal it when he speaks or when he writes. It is a pilgrim Spanish which Mister President of the continental newspaper men brings us. It has a certain exotic echo. No one can sort out from this Spanish the nasal speech of the people of lower Mississippi and the guttural rhythm of those born in the suburbs of Chicago. It is a noisy Spanish, the noise of what is foreign. It is the noise of the *English* underneath, and it *comes on top of us.*

* * *

A Yankee of this sort, or a Latin American of this sort, cannot stand alone. Jules Dubois is a man of important friendships in Latin capitals. Every time he comes to an airport, personages are on hand to greet him. As a rule

196

they are lordly gentlemen who speak English, learned also from disks and practiced at the Embassy receptions. The speech of this clan cannot conceal the transmigrated phonetic phrases that came to South America in the last century from Europe, and now travel on the rump of their English, from south to north, to rejoin related human fragments who emigrated in various epochs from Europe to North America. . . . What a rare spectacle there in the airports when Jules Dubois arrives: he intent on his mouthspray Baedeker Spanish; the others insisting on speaking their hybrid hissing English. The scene is illuminated with photographers' flash bulbs and interrupted by loud hemispheric guffaws. A few minutes later, a caravan of automobiles heads for the grand hotel, constructed by the functionaries who manipulate business and manage the factory.

Of all these friends and others, the one who loved Dubois most effusively, was paradigmatic Anastasio Somoza. Aside from the language (Somoza was formed politically in a North American business academy in Philadelphia), they were united by the new professional activity of managing the property of others. A strong Hispanic campaign was made with Somoza's money and in his behalf. Dubois restricted his trips to the Caribbean, where on every hand he eulogized that model of Police Rulers: that life-long custodian of imperialist "rights" for the (unnecessary) construction of a new Interoceanic Canal. But the eulogies for Somoza did not remain in the Caribbean. Dubois was barefaced enough to defend Somoza publicly in Montevideo at a congress of journalists—Somoza, his great hemispheric friend, whom a few Kommunists considered a dictator. Later, when Castillo Armas (shaped

197

commercially in the Yankee military academy at Fort Leavenworth), ruled Guatemala as a custodian for United Fruit,[13] another congress of newsmen had to endure his nasal dithyrambs in favor of Somoza. Perhaps there were protests against Dubois in Montevideo and Guatemala, but they must have been formulated in old-style Spanish. Dubois, Somoza, and Castillo Armas were not able to understand them, let alone pay any attention to them.

Dubois' friendship with Somoza served him privately and in SIP publicly. The syndicate needed to be respected and carry weight in Central American official circles. Somoza condescended to "elevate" SIP with the most extravagant solicitude: he asked that a delegation come to write the new law on freedom of the press (May, 1956). Apparently the Nicaraguan government had no politicians, no newsmen, no lawyers. For the first time, the hemispheric news syndicate was invited to exercise legislative powers. These are overwhelming testimonials of a voluntary submission to the Empire, but Somoza's obsequiousness did not have the "success" expected. SIP rejected Somoza's invitation because it did not wish any laws regulating the press. Not even if SIP itself could draw them up. "We do not wish any special law," the arrogant hemispheric newspapers have said on various occasions. The reason is that "freedom of the press is the right of every free man, hence needs no regulation." [14] By free men they mean those with enough dollars to start a big daily in which such a citizen and his principal "stockholders" can print whatever they wish. Unfortunately "free men" of this sort are very few in the United States and even fewer in Latin America. In the southern part of the hemisphere, rather than free men, there exist free

198

families, who have the right, and practice it, of setting forth, without any restrictions, their own opinions. The Gaínza Paz family and the Mitre family in Buenos Aires; the Batlle Pacheco and the Rodríguez Larreta family in Montevideo; the Edwards family in Valparaíso and Santiago; the Santos family in Bogotá; the Aramayo family in La Paz; the Miró Quesada family in Lima; the Arosemena family in Panama. However much we pad the list they will not reach fifty. And the result is that the governments of those Republics refrain from legislating on matters concerning commercial advertising. (The United States provides an example. "The Appeals Court of the State of Maryland declared unconstitutional a tax on newspaper advertisements, 'because it tends to limit the freedom of the press' and ordered $1,500,000 received in this manner be restored, according to *El País*, November 12, 1958.) In this way there will be no damage to the inalienable rights of these fifty powerful families, fraternally protected by equally free families there in the North. With the exception that there in the United States, the free millionaire families cannot be distributed by geographic zones. If one may speak of Pattersons and the McCormicks of Chicago and the Moors Cabots of Boston, the larger number operate throughout the country, such as the Scripps-Howard family, which alone has twenty-two daily papers. The Gannett family owns twenty-one. Farflung, too, is the rapid spread, like an oil stain, of those "editors" or "owners" or "directors" who are employed in dailies and magazines with the petroleum capital of the Rockefellers and the Pews, or also that other industrial empire of the House of Morgan. This last depended on and depends on the generalissimos, the big guns of publicity of the type of

Luce, Lamont, Lockett, and the heirs of Hearst. We also take note of the fact that there are consortiums and magazines controlled by them, such as Curtis Publishing (which had a Division General at its head: J. F. C. Fuller); Crowell Publishing and the International Paper Company. We cannot state that the enumeration of these free men, or free families or free consortiums, is inexhaustible. On the contrary, we scarcely need a page more to mention all of them.[15]

These talking millionaire families (the actual syndicate which Dubois heads) loudly demanded a Nazi government in 1936. A Nazi government and a military alliance with Hitler. We all know that under Hitler and Mussolini the press did not enjoy even elementary liberties. Then, when the political battle was lost, the North American Nazis took advantage of that defeat, they incorporated themselves as part of the "free world," and glorified the liberty which the Nazis and European Fascists had smashed down with clubs. From this day on, any law about publicity became repugnant. But this will be so only and exclusively when it tries to scratch free and unrestricted commercial publicity activity. A certain phrase by the Mayor of Bogotá when he spoke of press "liberty with responsibility" caused a light shiver in the renowned Argentine newspaperman Juan S. Valmaggia. See in *La Nación*, April 14, 1958, the article signed by Valmaggia with this eloquent title; "Every press law implies a restriction and conceals threats."

Special rancor is aroused by taxes on commercial advertising. Recall the case of Maryland. If the government imposes penny taxes on the advertisements of autos, cigarettes, miraculous patent medicines, and cosmetic creams . . . it is corrupting freedom of thought and is endangering culture!

Taking another step forward in this ideological throwback, better said in this *neo-Nazi fiction,* SIP came to set itself up as the supreme judge of the governments to the south, and the syndicate is the one that decides which one is dictatorial and which is democratic. The dictatorial and the democratic depend entirely on the treatment given to the owners of newspapers, to any one of the fifty families that speak English or the fifty families who speak Spanish. They do not accept laws: not even regulations.[16] Commercial publicity—that is to say, journalism—is a sacred function, like that of property, like international treaties, like . . . the cables of Mr. Hearst. And in their meddling career, they have come to threaten, from Washington, to overthrow any southern government which imposes "censorship of the press." [17] Press censorship is the one thing that characterizes dictatorial government. All governments which have tried to punish press organs promoting conspiracy or violating in other ways the fundamental laws of the state, have been labeled dictatorial. With this reservation: that the newspaper affected belongs to one of the free millionaire families of Latin America. If the daily paper or the publication belongs to an incorporated stock company infinitely democratized, depersonalized, or if it is a question of student magazines, workers' weeklies, organs of popular parties, then there is no defense and there is no offense; there is no dictatorship. In 1953 the President of Chile took measures against the person of the director of a Valparaíso daily: at once the voices of SIP in the North were heard. The daily belonged to a multimillionaire. Señor Presidente; don't be a vulgar dictator! Under the same Chilean government, on April 2, 1957, in Santiago, a printing plant, while the edifice was surrounded by police, was wholly destroyed in broad daylight. The plant did not belong to any particular family worthy of being defended. Señor Presidente: *you have served the cause of order!*

"We have been able to observe that, first with snarling threats, at times stupidly, and later brutally, the Law for the Defense of Democracy, was applied against Communism in a form that resulted in the unparalleled and ruthless destruction of a private print shop," commented *El Debate,* conservative daily, Santiago de Chile, May 25, 1957 in an editorial entitled *"Anticommunismo."*

President Velasco Ibarra, able and irascible, as a jurist, had to remind SIP on an occasion similar to that in Valparaíso, that Ecuador was *still* a sovereign Republic.

Perón, Rojas Pinilla, and Pérez Jiménez were branded there in the north, as being dictators, but only in the precise moment when they took measures against some newspapers in the SIP circuit.

Of Somoza, we already know that the Yankees were always benevolent.

Of Trujillo, North American opinion became divided only after he aroused the enmity of SIP by expropriating the newspaper *El Caribe.*

In contrast Batista was never called a dictator, because that able manufacturer of puffed-up militarists did not let a day go by without cultivating the millionaires of the Press, and he begged pardon of SIP every time an opposition newspaper man was killed. He never closed down a daily. Mostly he opened accounts for them in the banks. Censorship was transitory, with prior telegrams advising the United States of the step. English-speaking journalists were invited to the government's bilingual banquet. Everything else that occurred under the Batista regime, that spilled torrents of blood, did not upset the sensitivity of the directors of SIP.

Castillo Armas was never branded a dictator. He suppressed a valiant voice of the university students: *El Estudiante!* he expelled the directors, still adolescents, from the country. Two of them died right in the street from police bullets. SIP never said a word. *La Tribuna,* a good Aprista daily in Lima, and *El Pais,* voice of the majority party in Venezuela, were seized by the government for several years, their editors put in jail or in exile; SIP obstinately disregarded it. The actual Government of Bolivia, in contrast, is a dictatorship to a superlative degree, because it does not permit the publication of the daily newspaper *La Razón,* property of a certain family of free men, the *Aramayos,* victims ever since the "infamous nationalization" of their tin mines. The SIP journalists certainly know how to distinguish.

It is touching indeed, the passion demonstrated in behalf of freedom of thought by certain commercial enterprises in the United States. In May, 1957, a Newspaper Seminar of the Caribbean Zone was held in New Orleans. Again the commercial publicity and the philosophy of liberty. Again the dictatorships, their lawyers, journalists, business men, all together. But the costs of the Seminar were paid by . . . the United Fruit Company. See *El Mercurio,* May 9, 1957.

In the United States there was an effort to legislate against this thick *atole* gruel in which has been jumbled together the philosophy of freedom and the freedom to steal and lie. It was back in 1938 under the dictator Franklin Delano Roosevelt. The projected law went so far as to provide for the jailing of journalists (the chief purpose was the last) who lied in order to sell papers. The President of the United States opposed it. Not because of democratic principles or because of religious scruples, but because it was impractical. "There are not enough jails in the entire country," said the greatest of the governors of the United States in this twentieth century.[18]

Here to the south the situation is even more serious. SIP has interposed itself as a political entity between the governments on the one hand and the international association of newspaper industrialists, directed and protected by the United States. Some Latin American journalists are not absolutely sure about their true role; for others, in contrast, the Yankee patronage has generated a certain "professional" emotion, sufficiently embroidered with the hemispheric concept. So much so that they no longer have the slightest respect for their own governments. The aid extended from abroad to these time-servers is so great that their usual timidity has been replaced by a mysterious "political" courage, to such a degree that the subalterns feel a certain fulfillment in opposing the local authorities. They know that they have backing, and that the United States there in the metropolis has established a union of chosen journalists and interventionist scale of rewards. There, for the moment, is where Latin American journalists come to be crowned with laurels and remunerated. Columbia University in New York, for example, awards an annual Maria Moors Cabot prize, which, according to a Chilean journalist, is "the highest honor to which a

204

journalist of the hemisphere can aspire.[19] That is, it should be said, a foreign honor, since the one speaking is a Chilean. It should be added that it is a commercial reward, since the Moors Cabots are powerful stockholders of the United Fruit Company. But they have the excuse of having stamped on the prize the equivocal award: "The Hemisphere." When the hemisphere is spoken of, all outlines are blurred, colors become uniform in tone, frontiers are rubbed out. If these journalists were basically writers, they would never lose awareness of their native language, with which a writer expresses himself and perfects himself until he obtains the public applause of those who speak, read, and write the same language. But as this journalism, that is to say the art of fabricating and selling news has nothing to do with the language in which the news is printed, or in which the Standard Oil Company is eulogized, it is all the same whether it be celebrated in New York or in Buenos Aires. The "hemisphere" does not have its own language. Columbia University, furthermore, hastens to indicate that these prizes are handed out by newspaper companies "to promote international friendship in the Americas." And this international friendship is bilingual.

Unfortunately it is not merely a matter of friendship or of fabricating and selling news. Columbia University is interested in superior motives. It was the institution that bestowed on Castillo Armas the title of *Doctor Honoris Causa*. Castillo Armas was never a journalist; he never fabricated and sold news. Quite the contrary: he was fabricated as a personage and sold as news in a disastrous moment in international life.

Rómulo Gallegos [ex-President of Venezuela and a leading Latin American novelist] on learning that this honor had been given to the Colonel of the United Fruit, felt such disgust, since he had received the same award years before, that he returned it immediately with a letter that the Guatemalans will never forget. What Columbia University demands of the journalists and the Colonels is something more than publicity; it demands, for example, that the journalists and the Colonels endeavor to establish a sound economy in their countries; the first by means of opinions printed in the newspapers, the others by more striking methods, with their artillery, or from militarized public offices. A Chilean journalist merited the distinction from the Moors Cabot family for having defended in the columns of his paper "freedom of commerce." But still more: the Yankees decorated the Chilean journalist for having served "the national interests" (Chilean?) and for having served "the better understanding of the nations of the hemisphere." The journalist who accepted this honor as the highest reward at once traveled to New York to receive there in the city of high finance the material insignias and other marks of esteem. We do not know why, but right after the ceremonies at the University in New York, the journalist was taken to Washington . . . the Metropolis of . . . Diplomacy. Perhaps to be introduced to other journalists? No: to talk with the Minister of Colonies, a gentleman at that moment named Roy R. Rubottom.

Once he was in Washington, the prize was no longer of interest. Now the themes are: "the economic situation of Chile," the "anti-inflationist policy of the Chilean government," the disputes between the Chilean Congress and the President of the Republic, the electoral perspectives for the *presidential succession*, etc. Even with all this, the receptions (and the interrogation) did not terminate in Washington. The Latin American journalists, who permit themselves to be decorated by the Moors Cabot family, are obliged to return via Puerto Rico, to know at first hand this "factory of freedom," and ask Muñoz Marín himself how it is possible to govern a Latin nation with hemispheric and bilingual patriotism. The grateful journalist returns to his country of origin, and his declarations from this day on will have another technique, a different rhythm. Often the energy needed for these variations will not be overly great. In the case of the Chilean journalist to whom we are referring, we remember that already before receiving the award he had "directed appeals to the Government of the United States that it exercise its influence in *a more effective form*" to bring about better conditions of life for we sub-beings who live south of the Rio Grande.[20]

SIP, on its part, hands out rewards and titles no less honorific. The frequent visits of Jules Dubois to the countries of the Latin languages have enabled him to catalog the journalists who need stimulation. The prize given is called Mergenthaler, and is not financed by a free millionaire family of Boston, but by an industrial concern that manufactures and sells linotypes. Every year SIP gives five opportunities, and they are granted to "the Latin American journalist who distinguishes himself in his profession." It is noticeable that there is no interest in rewarding North Americans, no matter how much they stand out.

207

And it appears, the donors do not look for Colonels either. Sufficient are "the soldiers of the cause." We know that, in addition to the plane and railroad fares, lodging in chain hotels along the way and the well-known tips, the chosen journalist gets $500 in cash. There are those who won the trip for "having fought Communism," a stunt paid for in the United States at so much the line. This little theme greatly preoccupies the private industrialists and the millionaires of the State Department. On the other hand, it is a trifle strange in the case of journalists, the majority of whom are not millionaires.

But among so many instances, there was one that was symbolic. In October, 1954, the Brazilian journalist, Carlos Lacerda, manager of a daily paper, was Mergenthalized. According to a dispatch sent from Rio de Janeiro by the then agonizing "Agencia Latina" and published in the large dailies of Santiago de Chile on the 12th of October, Señor Lacerda, in addition to having been outstanding "in the exercise of his profession," merited this North American prize "for having fought corruption in the 'Brazilian' government." The reference was to the government of Getulio Vargas, who had ended his life by suicide the previous August, when the Army ordered him to resign. It was quite obvious that Lacerda had lent himself, as an inter-American journalist, to carrying out the foreign battle against the Creole "dictator." But note: the dictator left us a letter "written by his own hand," which was published by the Associated Press. Let us look at several paragraphs of that historic document:

> I follow the destiny imposed upon me. After years
> of domination and exploitation by economic and

financial groups, I became the head of an invincible revolution. . . . I began the work of liberation and instituted a regime of social emancipation. A subterranean campaign by international groups joined with the national groups working against the regime of guarantees for the workers. I fought against the exploitation of Brazil. I fought against the exploitation of the people. The hate, the infamy, and calumny did not break my spirit.[21]

The journalist Carlos Lacerda had played his part in this conspiracy of Yankee commercial interests and the "national" militarists against the President protecting the humble. After Vargas's death, Lacerda could say, using the language of a stock-exchange runner: "I believe that the country needs foreign capital and it will gladly accept it." [22] The prize from the United States was justified. SIP also knew how to fulfill its duty.

And SIP was also honored. After it had been playing an amphibian role as an "inter-American entity," the state of Delaware called it in to present it with a prize: that of registering it as a North American "corporation" under the laws of that state.[23] The Latin American journalists decorated by SIP shrugged their shoulders. They were unable to return the $500 or the tips. But a Mexican journalist, more as a Mexican than a journalist, felt such disgust that, in spite of being in charge of an SIP executive position, he resigned. A great sadness must have come over the spirit of Don Miguel Lanz Duret, the director of the daily paper, *El Universal*. After years of Inter-American labor, fatiguing trips, pouring out anti-Kommunism in streams, battling against numbers of dictators, opening closed doors, winning endless applause, decorations, too: he has finally had to admit that as journalists, we are subject to the laws of a Yankee state. SIP has a status analogous to that of the Panama Canal Zone, umbilically tied to the state of Illinois; to that of Puerto Rico, "The Free State," whose justice is subject to the high courts of Massachusetts. This was discussed in an article by Cesar Godoy Urrutia in *"El Estado Libre Asociado de Puerto Rico"* in *Orientación*, Santiago de Chile, December 6, 1957. Included in the article are the declarations of the illustrious Puerto Rican, Don Antonio Santaella Blanco, to the Brazilian Senate in June, 1957.

* * *

The free men of the United States (each of whom owns a big daily or a number of big dailies) who share with the free families of supercapitalist enterprise the publication of ads in papers and magazines which are distributed throughout the nation—or the free families of Latin America who do the same, investing in the business various millions accumulated during industrious generations —all those free men and free families exude an anti-Kommunism, suitable to the business and the profession of "owner of a newspaper," produced by the real or fictitious anxieties of the investor who wishes to increase his profits and to establish his rights to dividends in return for telling the truth, the whole truth, and nothing but the truth. Before this anti-Kommunism we bow down reverently, be the proprietor Mr. Hearst or be he named Miró Quesada, whether that ethical code and that journalistic credo is to our liking or not; whether our opinion coincides or not with that those journalists held of Franklin Delano Roosevelt. They would seem more respectable to us were we to recall that, after some years of conflict *precisely* with Roosevelt, the millionaire journalists came to an understanding with the Department of State, *precisely* when he died. When this came about, the powerful Wall Street office adopted as theirs the political ideas of Hitler and continued, in the English language, the salvationist crusade initiated twenty years before in Germany in a Munich beer hall.

The journalism of the enterprises, for this reason, is now anti-Kommunist, full beard and all. There is no reason for newspapers to be Kommunist or anti-Kommunist, but since it is a product of contemporary industry, it has to share the philosophy of the manufacturers. This type of journalism serves its own interests by being the antenna of the millionaires; and it serves the Department of State, another antenna of the millionaires. When we say, therefore, that the industrial journalists are the "geese of the Capitol," we say so without any desire to insult them for we know that they and the Capitol are identified with an economic philosophy and are motivated by the same pharasaical morality. *The Chicago Tribune* or the *Tribuna de Imprensa*—to mention only two megaphones— burst out in wild cackling every time it is convenient that a phantasmal submarine should appear (more phantom than submarine) in New York waters or those of the Río de la Plata, or whenever a Latin American government authorizes an increase in wages or legalizes strikes or propagates nationalism. All this is very well; it is to the point, it is timely, it has the proper rhythm. It is necessary

211

to defend . . . the Capitol. The people inside should be warned so that they awaken. The *Jus Latii*, Latinity, is in danger. And the duty of geese is to cackle.

We cannot confess to having this sort of respect for journalists who are not owners of the enterprise or do not belong to a millionaire family of enterprisers. That is to say: when we come to journalists who hire out their agility in hunting news, their ability as editors, and reedit their material to conform to the wishes of their bosses—who hire out their signature to dress up the articles of others, or point up news they did not bring in, or give comments not their own, and add to their hired signature their "integrity" in order that, when necessary, they will convert tripe into a heart and say: "Yes, gentlemen, I wrote that." In such odd cases, the journalists' posture loses meaning, and the value of the anti-Kommunism they declaim is also uttered, be it in their native land or in the United States at the moment they are honored by prizes from Moors Cabot or SIP. Of *this kind of* anti-Kommunists, also geese of the Capitol, we do not have the same respectful opinion. Nor in the United States are they held in great esteem. A certain idiomatic pride prevents me from repeating the epithets, in English and in Castilian, which are used to stigmatize such types of journalists. We content ourselves with the knowledge that there, as here, they are not respected, perhaps because they have no respect for themselves either.

These are second-rank journalists, an ill-defined kind of geese, geese now, but later on they may become different birds. If the legitimate geese are allowed at the portals, these improvised geese are assigned a place well outside the gardens, or they are hidden in the pens, or they are kept at one side of the pool. A sense of hierarchy, instinctive in every millionaire, counsels that they are kept at a distance. Moreover, their cackles should not go above certain notes; their precarious musical scale is delimited. Their cackles must not be confused with other cackles. The people of the palace must be able to know when the important geese and when those others, the hired geese, cackle. The different cackles indicate different dangers. When the owner of newspapers cackles, the submarine is a very large one, and it is more Russian. When the cackle is from the second-line geese, the submarine can scarcely be seen and is almost English.

*　　*　　*

Nature displays infinite variety as a sign of its creative power. And the varieties of geese number more than two. There are also geese of the Capitol in a third sense: certain human specimens neither millionaires nor stockholders, who do not hire out their editorial talents, who do not practice journalism of any sort, who have no public position, and whose connections or bosses are not visible. The North American Ambassadors possess the merit of having discovered these geese, of having "selected" them (an upside down selection), of having attracted and persuaded them, of having altered their attire to make them appear uniformed on the outside and inside, and having given them an imperial passport so they are not held up at any frontier. They are geese of a different plumage and for other waters. Not for the garden pool, but for running waters, the useful waters, for navigating upstream and

213

downstream, for the rapids, not for tame waters. These are traveling geese, who gather in flocks at the point designated to beat their flightless wings and cackle in unison. Because of their awkward waddle they cannot be mistaken.

I refer to the professional anti-Kommunists, who are not really anti-Kommunist—the adjective does not properly apply for they are substantive anti-Kommunists, the substance being the dollar which inspires them. They have made anti-Kommunism their profession of faith, identifying it with the subsistence ration by which they survive. There are one or two dozen of this subspecies in every Latin American country, and they are organized with an executive committee in which naturally there is never lacking a treasurer. From modest individual contributions, so small that they are invisible, they have managed to amass in New York certain funds which make it possible for them to travel frequently, to put up at the best hotel in the city, to have at their disposal theaters for their meetings, to enjoy profuse newspaper publicity and appear in expensive movie "shorts." They put out elegant magazines and books with no publishing house indicated. These are the neo-anti-Kommunists. These are the *neo-geese*. That is what they are for: to cackle while on the wing. Pardon: to fly cackling. They do not cackle because their own millions, which they will never have, are in danger, but because the millions belonging to others are in danger. But between the millions of others and their own nonexistent millions, there is a mathematical relationship, and it is all-important. If those millions should disappear or be reduced, their salaries would also disappear, along with the twenty-story hotel, the photographs in the large dailies, the four-motor airplanes.

Up until the moment of writing these lines, the neo-geese of anti-Kommunism have met in four Roman-style congresses and in one . . . Athenian style Forum. I shall discuss briefly here the first three of these congresses. Of the fourth congress held in Guatemala in 1958 I do not yet have enough documentation. The Anti-Kommunist Forum held in Montevideo in September, 1958, we shall have the opportunity of discussing on another occasion. The first of these congresses was convened in Mexico City in May, 1954, on the eve of the Guatemalan invasion. The theme of the Congress, naturally, was the Guatemalan Revolution, its ties with Russia, the danger for the Panama Canal, and for the Las Vegas atomic secrets. We have already seen in a previous chapter that Doctor Uribe y Misas was the ecclesiastical contribution to the reunion. The Vice President of the sessions was a Guatemalan, a lawyer for the United Fruit Company. His name: Carlos Salazar Gatica (C.S.G.). He was the first Minister of Foreign Affairs of Castillo Armas and later became the Finance Minister of Ydígoras Fuentes. In this new post, he has been able to carry out a typical anti-Kommunist exploit: He *pardoned* the United Fruit a debt of two million dollars, which that peculiar enterprise owed but had never paid to the State. Salazar Gatica has not invented anything new. Another anti-Kommunist government in Honduras, that of General Carías Andino, pardoned the poverty-stricken company a debt contracted in 1933 and in 1947 for the laughable sum of 92 million dollars. Thus the reader can understand why the United Fruit is able to shell out for fares, hotels, and tips to those attending Press Seminars and anti-Kommunist Congresses.

The second Congress chose as its theater the city of Rio

de Janeiro and was held in August, 1955, to celebrate, without doubt, the first anniversary of the suicide of Vargas. Also Brazil was on the eve of elections. The popular forces, vengeful as always, wished to return the followers of Getulio Vargas to power. The army, for its part, was prepared to prevent this. For this purpose, a Congress that would let loose a monotonous geese-cackle warning of the Kommunist danger (Getulio Vargas, Adhemar de Barros, Juscelino Kubitschek, all unpardonable Kommunists) and of the necessity that somebody save the Fatherland, would be most useful. Present in the Congress to talk about the Fatherland, the Patria, was a retired Brazilian admiral. But the *vedette* of this second Congress was the Mexican, Florencio Avila Sánchez, who claimed to represent Nelson Rockefeller and Castillo Armas, rated (Sánchez, i.e.) as a "continental figure." [24] More modest was the participation of ex-Senator Sergio Fernández Larraín, the one who has undertaken the arduous task of cataloging all the Kommunists of Chile, in *Sergio Fernández Larraín Informa*, a book of 180 pages (Santiago de Chile), 1954. The Congress closed without the Brazilian army having given the *cuartelazo* asked for by the oligarchy. Kubitschek was elected. Immediately the best known geese reappeared: Carlos Lacerda called upon the army not to recognize the results of the election and seize power, according to *El Dia*, Montevideo, October 15 and 18, 1955. [Lacerda, now governor of the province that includes Rio de Janeiro, is the most brutal of the anti-Kommunists now at large in Latin America, a Fascist by conviction and methods, and also, as one might expect, the supreme pet of the State Department.—Translator] Luckily on this occasion, army opinion was divided.

The third Latin American anti-Kommunist Congress met in Lima in April, 1957. It produced surprises scarcely Latin American: "Russian observers," an observer for Nationalist China, and a pair of Hungarian survivors from 1956. The Cuban delegate, Señor De la Fe, said to work for the F.B.I., proposed the creation of a continental army, coupled to the Organization of American States. From Brazil by land, without even "making water," came Admiral Penna Botto. And with him reappeared one of the great ones of these Congresses, the Chilean writer, Lautaro Silva Cabrera, personal friend of Generalissimo Trujillo, the generous donor. This writer, whose pen is perhaps the best paid for in the Caribbean—without his being a Carib —traveled on to Guatemala accompanied by a charming young Chilean poetess. As was customary, they solicited funds to publish a book against Kommunism. This book, which had already cost Trujillo some thousands of dollars, was revised by Castillo Armas, who gave the money requested, but with one objection: "A chapter about Arévalo is lacking." The poet and the poetess had to wait various hours, while the amanuenses of Castillo Armas prepared the pages for the new chapter. Some day we may know this much traveled costly book.

POPULAR WRITER ARRESTED IN LOS
CERILLOS. GIGANTIC CONTRABAND OF
WATCHES. TRAVELER ACCOMPANIED BY
THE FAMOUS POETESS MARIA CHRISTINA
MENARES: $5,000,000.

With the cruelty natural to millions, the daily *Clarín* of Santiago "sold" this news on September 15, 1957. The author of the account, a friend of Lautaro Silva Cabrera, a colleague of his in good literature but not in evil habits, did not wish to print the full name of the man involved.

The contraband came from Africa. It reached the airport of the Chilean capital "in two suitcases carried by the writer L.S." The "said" writer, reported the chronicler, was traveling "in the company of the celebrated poetess María Christina Menares." "The sleuths of the International Investigation Police," also anti-Kommunist . . . had no other recourse than to examine the watches and to initiate at that exact moment the customary procedure against what is known in Castilian as *contrabando*. In gracious anticipation of the writers' return, on July 28 of that same year, *La Nación* of Santiago, had published the photograph of these two personages of the Customs as they were then being received by Castillo Armas. In the *La Nación's* photograph, there also appears the Guatemalan Goose, Roberto Castañeda, who was to become famous later on for having manufactured a "life diary" of the little soldier to whom, from the first moment, it had been convenient to attribute the assassination of Castillo Armas. Gentlemen of industry, smugglers, forgers, traitors of the country . . . all are pure gold: anti-Kommunists. Even the photograph is worth gold!

That third congress was arranged, as that in México, as that in Brazil, to solve some immediate political problem. This time the problem was *Bolivia*. Its mass revolution, disrespectful of sacred property, disrespectful of the freedom of opinion of the Aramayo family, was obviously Kommunist. Siles Suazo, who had already staged two hunger strikes, did not feel strong enough to continue the fight and decided to solve things in a friendly fashion. He asked the [anti-Kommunist] Congress (as Somoza did the

SIP) to come to Bolivia to investigate the facts. Those of the Third Congress, neither slow nor lazy, designated a seven-man commission, several of whom were installed within days in the Hotel Sucre as the guests of a cowed government. They ate, they drank, they danced. Accompanied by the men of the regime, they had the whim of conversing with enemies of Siles Suazo. Thus by getting possession of documents of every sort, they were able to pick out those which strengthened the anti-Kommunist thesis of the congress. They prepared a report, published as a book in Santiago de Chile.[25] Carlos Simons (C.S.) a Guatemalan, a famous employee of United Fruit, though a member of the commission, could not go to Bolivia, but his name appears among those signing the report "as if" he had actually been in Bolivia.

Another novelty in the Third Congress: it was agreed to form an "Inter-American Association of Anti-Kommunist Journalists." This, it was later explained, was *to prevent journalism from being prostituted.*[26]

With names like the Chilean writer L.S. and with employees of the United Fruit such as C.S. and C.S.G., obviously journalism will never be prostituted. These are the moralists of the Hearst line, the soldiers of reaction, like Jules Dubois, soldier of Somoza. Thus, we cannot make bad auguries about the fate of this puritanical entity. Biology teaches us that certain bacilli can be utilized to create fermentation. The peasants of the whole world use human excrements to combat the effect of snake-bite. From dirty petroleum comes healthful vaseline. A mangy mess, A-377, serves as the base of aureomycin. In my presence, a famous Chilean doctor in a restaurant ate rotten peaches and confessed he preferred them to sound ones.

219

I recall, from Mendoza days, the best of all examples. The erudite Italian, Doctor Julio Savastano, a technical authority on olive culture and a colleague of mine at the University of Cuyo, suggested to the municipal authorities —that was about 1943—a scientifically sound project of using on surrounding fields the black waters, which come out of sewers thick as molasses—excellent waters, insisted the scholar—to fertilize land for the planting of olive trees. In this way, the finest olives in the world would be obtained. I do not know if the Mendoza stores and markets are provided with meaty, juicy, rich olives such as those promised by Savastano. But with the same art and similar magic, could not "hemispheric" journalism take new moral and unsullied paths by utilizing those men who—like heavy waters are poured over Latin America—now cackle in unison with the money provided by the Police State rulers and the uncorruptible United Fruit Company?

NOTES TO CHAPTER V

1. *El Siglo* (Santiago de Chile), November 12, 1955.

2. Seldes, *Los Amos de la Prensa* (Lords of the Press) (1st Spanish ed., Buenos Aires, n.d.), p. 271.

3. *Ibid.* Read the whole work: Gregorio Selser is preparing a complete edition with notes. In the later work by Seldes, *Mil Americanos, Los Dictadores de Los Estados Unidos*, these topics are amplified.

4. *El Mercurio*, October 28, 1954.

5. *Ibid.*, December 31, 1955.

6. Brady, p. 354. In addition, the two works of Seldes already cited are veritable encyclopedias of the numerous infamies of this nature which have been committed in the United States.

7. Félix Gordón Ordaz. *Hacia una Revisión de Nuestra*

Política en el Exilio (Toward a Revision of Our Policy in Exile) (Paris, 1955), p. 25.

8. *El País* (Montevideo), August 1, 1958.

9. In Santiago de Chile in 1952, during the First World Congress of Newspapermen, Latin American journalists, those who faithfully carry on their profession, supported the Uruguayan resolution on Freedom of the Press, the second section of which denounced "the financing of periodical enterprises by means of *secret sources* alien to the public interest." The text went on to refer to the "subsidies and commercial advertising" which corrupt the free emission of news and comments. Luís Oribe Alemany, "Estados Unidos bajo la Cortina de Hierro e Impidio Reunirse a los Periodistas" (The United States Lowered the Iron Curtain and Prevented the Reunion of Newspaper Men) , *Jornada* (Montevideo), May 17, 1956.

10. See my two articles in *Marcha* (Montevideo): "El Gran Provocador, mister Nixon" (The Great Provocateur, Mr. Nixon) , May 30, 1958; and "Buenas Noches, Tristeza" (Sad Goodnight) [re Dulles' visit to Brazil], August 8, 1958.

11. Cf. Gregorio Selser, "Jules Dubois, Corresponsal Viajero" (Jules Dubois, Traveling Correspondent), *Propósitos* (Buenos Aires) , February, 1957.

12. Dardo Cuneo, Prologue in the book of José Martí, *Argentina y la Primera Conferencia Panamericana* (Buenos Aires, 1955), p. 12.

13. Jules Dubois, married to a Panamanian and once declared *persona non grata* by the Panamanian government, with the Reserve rank of Colonel instructed Latin Americans at the Chief of Staff school of the academy mentioned, and it was precisely in that epoch that Castillo Armas took his finishing studies (around 1947).

14. *El Mercurio,* May 5, 1956; La Nación (Buenos Aires) , April 14, 1958.

15. Read all of the two thick books by Seldes previously cited here.

16. *El Mercurio,* April 8, 1956.

17. "Noticias de Ultima Hora" (Santiago de Chile) , October 18, 1957.

18. Seldes, *Lords of the Press*, p. 388.

19. *El Mercurio*, October 23, 1957.

20. *Ibid.*, October 22, 1957.

21. *Ibid.*, August 25, 1954.

22. *Ibid.*, September 30, 1954.

23. *Ibid.*, April 8, 1958.

24. *Diario Ilustrado* (Santiago de Chile), July 29, 1955.

25. *Marxismo en Bolivia* (Marxism in Bolivia) (Santiago de Chile, 1957) , 287 pp. The book does not show the name of the editor or printer.

26. *El Mercurio*, May 9, 1957.

INDEX

224